from

OLD HOLLYWOOD

to

NEW BRUNSWICK

Memories of a Wonderful Life

CHARLES FOSTER

NIMBUS
PUBLISHING

I would like to put on record my appreciation of the brilliant and intelligent work done by my Nimbus editor, Whitney Moran. Her research and concern for accuracy has undoubtedly enhanced the content of my book. I consider her participation a great asset to the completed book.

—Charles Foster

—⟋⟋⟋—

Library and Archives Canada Cataloguing in Publication

Foster, Charles, 1923–, author
From old Hollywood to New Brunswick :
memories of a wonderful life / Charles Foster.

Includes bibliographical references and index.
Issued in print and electronic formats.
ISBN 978-1-77108-072-9 (pbk.).—ISBN 978-1-77108-073-6 (pdf).
ISBN 978-1-77108-075-0 (mobi).—ISBN 978-1-77108-074-3 (epub)

1. Foster, Charles, 1923-. 2. Public relations consultants—United States—Biography. 3. Celebrities—Public relations—United States. 4. Screenwriters—United States—Biography. 5. Speechwriters—Canada—Biography. 6. Journalists—New Brunswick—Biography. 7. Performing arts—United States—History. 8. Hollywood (Los Angeles, Calif.)—Biography. I. Title.

HM1226.F67 2013   659.2'092   C2013-903456-0
                                  C2013-903457-9

Nimbus Publishing acknowledges the financial support for its publishing activities from the Government of Canada through the Canada Book Fund (CBF) and the Canada Council for the Arts, and from the Province of Nova Scotia through the Department of Communities, Culture and Heritage.

On the Cover
Jimmy Edwards (lower left) and Benny Hill (top right) were guests of my wife, Irene, and I at a banquet in London in the 1950s. I met Jimmy while in the RAF in Moncton and Benny Hill on Central Pier in Blackpool, England, where he was beginning his fabulous career in 1952.

CONTENTS

PROLOGUE

It was on Thursday, July 16, 1936, that I first realized Atlantic Canada existed. On that memorable day, a very important Atlantic Canadian who had reached his pinnacle of success in England spent more than two hours extolling the wonders of this unique part of North America to a very unimportant person, me.

Born William Maxwell Aitken in Maple, Ontario, in 1879, his family had moved to Newcastle, New Brunswick, when he was under a year old. It was there he published his first newspaper when he was only thirteen. He graduated with honours from high school in Newcastle and had registered at Dalhousie University and King's College but did not attend either. He attended the University of New Brunswick briefly before quitting to become a clerk in the Chatham, New Brunswick, office of lawyer Richard Bennett, who later became prime minister of Canada. A visit to Halifax when he was eighteen introduced Aitken to John F. Stairs, who gave him a job in the Stairs family's finance business. When Stairs died in 1904, Aitken, who had demonstrated an astonishing ability to handle huge financial undertakings, took over the company, Royal Securities.

In 1906 Max Aitken married Haligonian Gladys Drury. It was a happy marriage that lasted, sadly, only until 1927, when Gladys died from cancer at age forty-one. By then, the Aitkens, having made a great deal of money in Halifax in a variety of Canadian financial ventures, were in London, England, where Aitken had shown that Atlantic Canadians were equal in brainpower to anyone anywhere in the world. He had taken over one of England's national daily newspapers, the *Daily Express*, when it was foundering. By changing the paper's entire policy he'd made it the largest and most successful in the country, with a circulation of more than three million copies per day.

Aitken had also become a MP for Ashton-under-Lyne in Lancashire and in business became a major shareholder in the growing Rolls-Royce Ltd. During the First World War he had been put in charge of the Canadian War Records Office and was knighted in 1911 by King George V for his work to strengthen England. But he did not forget his Canadian roots. During the war he took charge of recording the success stories of Canadians and made sure they were well publicized in both Britain and Canada. By this time Aitken owned four British newspapers, including the *London Evening Standard*. In 1917, as a result not only of his business successes but for his quiet generosity and good work for those in need, Aitken was elevated to the peerage. As Lord Beaverbrook, he took his seat in the prestigious British House of Lords.

Why I, in 1936, at the age of thirteen, was talking to this remarkable gentleman is a proud memory I will recall later. But my introduction to the wonders of Atlantic Canada began on a very rough sea trip from Dover in Kent, England, to Calais, France, as I sat beside Lord Beaverbrook en route to yet another country—Germany—where something very important was about to take place.

Lord Beaverbrook was the first Atlantic Canadian I had ever met. But to this day, I remember him telling me that despite his successes in England nowhere else in the world would ever eclipse his memories of New Brunswick and Nova Scotia. "You must go there one day," he said. "If you do, tell them I will one day do something to say thank you for the start I received there in my life."

He certainly kept that promise. After the Second World War ended, Lord Beaverbrook became chancellor of the University of New Brunswick and while in Fredericton, apart from many large donations to the university, he funded the building of the Beaverbrook Art Gallery and filled it with priceless art. He also built the Fredericton Playhouse, the Lord Beaverbrook Hotel, and the Lady Beaverbrook Arena. He provided millions for scholarships to the university, and spread his generosity to places like the Miramichi where he built the Lord Beaverbrook Arena. A school in Campbellton, New Brunswick, exists because he gave the city the funds, and his foundation of the Beaverbrook Chair in Ethics and Communications at McGill University came from his love of Canada and of Canadians. It would take a lot more space to include all his other efforts to say thank you to Atlantic Canada, but it must be included that Saint John still boasts the Lord Beaverbrook Rink.

During the Second World War, Seven years after meeting Lord Beaverbrook, I visited New Brunswick. In 1943 the Royal Air Force (RAF) shipped me across the Atlantic to New York on the mighty *Queen Elizabeth*, and from there we travelled by train to 31 Personnel Dispatch Centre in Moncton, where we awaited our turn to be sent out west for flight training. It was my experience in Moncton during those six weeks that brought me back again in 1970 for what I anticipated would be another six weeks.

After forty-three years I am still here.

My wife and I have enjoyed every day of those years and have told many people, including our son, Ian, that nowhere else in the world offers the friendliness and opportunities of Atlantic Canada. Ian and his wife, Sheila, moved here five years ago and are now spreading the same enthusiasm for our region.

I haven't made the millions that Lord Beaverbrook achieved, nor have I contributed to this part of the world as he later did, but I have learned that what he told me in 1936 is absolutely correct: Atlantic Canada is undoubtedly the best place in the world to live. Since that first meeting with Lord Beaverbrook. I have talked to many other expatriate Atlantic Canadians. One who stands out is the man who made Metro-Goldwyn-Mayer (MGM) Studios in Hollywood the most illustrious and lasting of all time: Louis B. Mayer. I recall Mayer telling me it was the work ethic he learned in his father's scrap metal yard in Saint John, New Brunswick, that taught him compassion for other workers and showed him many more abilities not learned in school—like concern for every employee—that made him successful in Hollywood.

I met actor Harold Russell, from Sydney, Nova Scotia, in 1972 when I found myself seated next to him at an afternoon Boston Red Sox game. *The Best Years Of Our Lives* was an Academy Award-winning film in 1947, and permitted Russell to become the only person in film history to win two Oscars for the same role. He was awarded the Academy Award for Best Supporting Actor, and, as a veteran in the United States Army who had lost his arms in a wartime tragedy, an additional, Honorary Oscar for bringing hope and courage to fellow veterans.

Because I was from New Brunswick, Russell invited me to spend that evening at his home in nearby Wayland, Massachusetts, to meet his wife and family. He used that evening to extol his home country and Nova Scotia. "I'm American now," he said, "But the Canadian way of life I learned at school in Nova Scotia made me the man I am today, and gave me my ability to weather disaster and come out smiling."

Two Broadway stars, Christie MacDonald, from Pictou, Nova Scotia, and Donald Brian, from St. John's, Newfoundland, both spent a lot of time sharing with me their memories of Atlantic Canada. Both were proud to tell me that it was their Canadian educators who gave them the strength to work harder when failure seemed inevitable, and that those people were responsible—much more than all the producers and directors—for the fame and enjoyable lives MacDonald and Brian lived.

Ruby Keeler, another Broadway star from Halifax, and her good friend, actor David Manners (also from Halifax), had nothing but good memories of Atlantic Canada. Ruby told me: "There are no other people in the world as kind as Haligonians. I have many friends around the world, but the ones I must never lose are those I knew when my life was just beginning."

David Manners told me one night of friends in Halifax he had been able to help on their way to success. "But I would never want their names publicized, because one is now a renowned hotel owner and does not like to recall the rough days of his youth. But I have never forgotten my Canadian friends. I have many friends now, but those from Nova Scotia were and still are my real friends."

I could add the words of Donald Sutherland, Fay Wray, Jack Cummings, George Cleveland, Henry Beckman, Edward Earle, Wallace MacDonald, Walter Pidgeon, Gordon Pinsent, Joe and Sam De Grasse, and producer Harry Saltzman, for all these successful people made it quite clear that it was the education and family life of Atlantic Canada that gave them the impetus to know they could succeed in life.

I have been extremely fortunate in my life. I have been privileged to meet kings, queens, presidents, princes, dukes, earls, and countless celebrities. Many remained friends for life. Unfortunately, too many have now left this earth.

My schooling ended at thirteen when I ran away to join a circus. Despite this lack of formal education, I was able to pass the aircrew examination that university students were flunking, and at eighteen was accepted as a pilot trainee in the British Royal Air Force. I graduated with my wings in Canada in 1943 when I was just twenty. I wrote comedy for giants like Bob Hope, Jimmy Edwards, Benny Hill, and Jack Benny, and for the best television comedy series in Hollywood, back when comedy was clean and funny. But that was a long time ago. So why did I have all this great fortune? I have always believed the answer is very simple: I was in the right place at the right time.

Though it was unpleasant at the time, I now realize the most important place of all was the Colonel Belcher Hospital in Calgary, Alberta, during the Second World War—for it was there I was befriended by Peter Middleton, the man I always consider the one person responsible for making my entire career and life possible. Only recently did I discover that Peter was an even more important man in the life of one of today's most delightful, talked about, photographed, and impressive persons who will be on the world's front pages long after I have left this earth. (The story of Peter Middleton's influence on my entire life is in chapter one.)

Looking back now, I have no doubt that the best of all these "right" places is the town of Riverview, New Brunswick, which I have happily called home for more than forty-three years.

I can proudly say that since I joined the circus at thirteen I have never once been out of work, nor once claimed employment insurance. Thanks to the work I chose to do, I have travelled extensively around the Atlantic provinces; and like those renowned people I met, I have nothing but praise for the friendliness of people of all walks of life in the communities I have visited.

I celebrated my sixty-fifth wedding anniversary this year. Over the years, my wife and I have together visited twenty-eight countries around the world including most of Europe and South America an exotic places like Hong Kong and Singapore. Today, with most of our travelling over, we just walk three kilometres around the block every morning after breakfast giving treats to every tail-wagging dog we meet. And we thank our lucky stars that somehow we ended up in Atlantic Canada.

IN 1943 I MET THE MAN
WHO CHANGED MY LIFE

I had just completed my twelve-week training course at 32 Elementary Flying Training School (EFTS), at Bowden, north of Calgary. As one of the top graduates of this preliminary pilot's course, I had been posted to 37 Service Flying Training School (SFTS) in nearby Calgary, where I was to fly the powerful single-engine Harvard aircraft.

Together with the other trainees at Bowden, I had visited Calgary on a number of occasions, and I looked forward to spending a few months in the great city. Our advanced training school was based at what is now Calgary International Airport. In those days it was a very small airport seemingly miles from the heart of the city. A couple days after arriving, we were all introduced to our new instructors. I was a little astonished when I met the man allocated to me. I discovered he was just three years older than me, but figured he wouldn't be there if he hadn't the qualifications to teach me all I needed to know to earn my pilot's wings.

Because of his youth, Peter Middleton was a little different than the other instructors. The officers—and Peter was a flying officer—usually expected us mere leading aircraftmen (LACs) to call them "sir." Even the non-commissioned pilots expected to be given that same honour. Peter made it clear from the first day we went up in the noisy Harvard that I was to call him Peter. "No 'sir,'" I recall him telling me, "We're all in this together; let's be friends."

I began to look forward to my days in the air with Peter. His attitude gave me confidence, and after only a week I was convinced that, despite his youth, I had very likely found the best instructor the RAF had ever produced.

But my training ended almost as soon as it began. After only ten days, I developed a fever and a temperature of 104° F. On arrival at the base hospital I was diagnosed with scarlet fever. Two days later I was moved to the Colonel Belcher Hospital in Calgary because I was showing signs of an even worse problem: rheumatic fever. If you don't know anything about rheumatic fever—which, happily, is rare these days—it gives its sufferers the most agonizing pains in every part of his or her body.

While I was quarantined with scarlet fever I was allowed no visitors at the Belcher, but when it turned into rheumatic fever alone, I was allowed to have friends drop by. The first person to visit me was Peter Middleton, the man I was just getting to respect when my flying days had ended abruptly. "After you went into hospital, I packed all your things in your kit bag," he said. "You don't have to worry about anything. Everything will be there when you get out of here."

Peter and I became great friends. He visited almost every day for the six weeks I spent in the Belcher. Many days he brought friends I had trained with at Bowden. They sat by my bed and tried hard to get me to forget the terrible pain that was with me twenty-four hours a day. Peter was honest enough to tell me the doctors feared my heart might possibly be affected, and that it could well be the end of my flying days—and possibly the end of my RAF days. But he took the trouble to investigate the illness thoroughly and he was able to encourage me with stories of other sufferers who had completely recovered. He urged me not to give up hope.

One of the things that helped me through those agonizing weeks in hospital was a morning radio program from station CFCN in Calgary. Frank Eckersley, the announcer, always started his two-hour show at 7 AM with a swingy version of the "Blue Danube" by Ray Noble and His Orchestra. I loved the big band sound of that era and listened every morning, hoping Mr. Eckersley would play a new Glenn Miller or Benny Goodman or Artie Shaw record that I had not heard before.

Peter began to realize what a big role this morning program was playing in my recovery. So he went down to the radio station, talked to

Frank Eckersley, and gave him a list of all my favourite songs, singers, and bands, and explained that I desperately needed a boost to get me out of the depression I had sunken into at the hospital.

Frank Eckersley responded.

One glorious morning, I heard my name called as the program went on the air: "Charles Foster, this program is for you. Your friend Peter Middleton has told me about your illness and the pain you are suffering. Both of us hope the music you are about to hear will help get you out of hospital soon."

For two hours Eckersley played every tune I wanted to hear, talked about the bands, and told me secrets about the singers and musicians. From that day on I called him Dr. Frank Eckersley, for from that day on I started to recover.

Peter was delighted. "So what are you going to do with the leave you will get when you get out of hospital?" he asked. I told him I had once dreamed of visiting Hollywood and had a letter in my kit bag addressed to Sir Charles Aubrey Smith, the renowned British actor then living in Hollywood. He had been a schoolmate of my father at Malvern College in Worcestershire, England. "But I don't think I'll have the strength to tackle a journey like that," I said. "It has always been a dream to see Hollywood, but maybe I'll just stay in Calgary and take it easy until I can get back to flying."

Peter wasn't sold on that idea. He kept nagging me about going to Hollywood. "If you have a friend there, go and see him," he said. "Leave everything to me. But first I think I can get you a two-week stay at the Harrison Hot Springs Hotel in British Columbia. It has been turned into a convalescent hospital for people in the armed forces. A couple of weeks there and you'll have your strength back before you know it. How does that sound?"

Of course it sounded wonderful. Anything out of the hospital sounded wonderful—although I must put on record that the doctors, nurses, and other staff members at the Colonel Belcher Hospital had been superb during my long stay with them. I made many friends there but I was more than ready to get back to the world outside.

"I will arrange to collect all your back pay," added Peter. "I'll have it ready for you when you return to Calgary from Harrison Hot Springs. I've already looked after your kit and personal things, so you won't have to do a thing except collect that letter to Sir Aubrey Smith, get on the train, and head into the sunshine of California." I found it hard to believe that one man would go so far out of his way to help another man he really hardly knew, but thanks to the concern of Peter Middleton, I actually began to feel hopeful that I had a future.

Finally, the pains subsided. Peter had kept his word. Everything was set for me to go to Harrison Hot Springs for two weeks to recuperate. The hotel turned out to be amazing. In peacetime it had been a luxury spa, but now it was full of servicemen getting over various serious medical problems. For some happy reason, Mr. Gusseme, the hotel owner, was still running the entire operation. He put me in charge of the library, which allowed me to spend my days selecting appropriate books for the other residents before taking every afternoon off to walk around the beautiful grounds.

Peter called the hotel every day to ask the doctors how I was progressing. At the end of the first week, he actually came up from Calgary by train and spent a day encouraging me to look forward to the future. He was an incredible man. "I'll meet you at the rail depot when you get back, drive you to the base to pick up what you need, and I already have a train ticket for you from Calgary to Spokane in Washington. There you will be able to get another train that will take you all the way to your destination, Hollywood. Are you going to be fit enough to tackle the trip?" His enthusiasm worked. I said I would be ready. With Peter's determination and my belief that I had apparently conquered rheumatic fever with no heart complications, I suddenly believed the future was beginning to look bright again.

Mr. Gusseme drove me to the train depot in Harrison Hot Springs. When I arrived at Calgary's main rail station, Peter was there with Gwen, a nurse from the Belcher. They drove me to No. 37, where I picked up all the things I needed for my vacation. Peter had arranged my leave pass. Twenty-one days sounded incredibly glorious. He gave me my back pay: four hundred dollars Canadian plus one hundred in US currency. Where the US dollars came from I never knew. He and

Gwen handed me a rail ticket from Calgary to Spokane and ignored my urging that I pay for it. Then, as a final gesture, he and Gwen drove me to the Palliser Hotel—Calgary's finest. "We've booked a room for you here tonight," said Peter. "It will be a taste of the luxury we hope you will find in Hollywood at the home of your father's friend. Have your supper—everything is paid—and I'll be here at eight in the morning to take you to the station and put you on the train."

Peter was one of only two men I met in my entire life who never broke a promise. (I'll tell you about the other much later.) The next morning he saw me safely on board the train before he headed back to 37 SFTS, where some fortunate young student was awaiting the benefit of his outstanding flying knowledge. My entire wonderful life started that day when Peter put me on the train to Spokane. What my life would have been like had he not been enthused enough to encourage me to face the world after my hospital stay, I shall never know.

Because of Peter's determination, I got to Hollywood.

I met so many wonderful people and made enough memories in Hollywood to convince me to make a success of my life. Many of the people I met back in 1943 would become a major part of my future. But there is something I discovered only this past summer about Peter Middleton. When Prince William (one day to be king of England) and his beautiful wife, Princess Catherine (Kate), arrived in Canada to enchant us with their positive outlook for the future and their completely down-to-earth way of looking at life the delightful Princess Catherine announced that she hoped, while on their visit to Calgary, to see the airport where her grandfather had once been an instructor in the RAF Commonwealth Air Training Program. Yes, Peter Middleton, the man who made my enjoyable life possible, was the grandfather of Catherine Middleton, one day to be the queen of England.

Perhaps you should all take a look back at those people who, in the past, helped your lives in any way. They should never be forgotten. I doubt you will ever have the good fortune to meet one as generous and concerned as was Peter Middleton all those years ago, but hopefully looking back will help you create a few wonderful memories of your own.

Thank you, Peter. This book and my life are dedicated to you.

SIDNEY AND VALENTINE OLCOTT: PROUD CANADIANS IN HOLLYWOOD

The journey to Los Angeles was so uneventful, I must confess I snoozed on and off most of the way, still not fully recovered from my hospital stay. It was early evening when the train pulled into the railroad depot, and I walked outside the station into a world I had always dreamed of seeing. After finding a telephone box I called the number of Sir Aubrey Smith. His phone was answered immediately by a very English voice. Things were on track: I had found my father's old friend.

"Sir," I said. "My father was Charles Foster. You went to school with him at Malvern College and he gave me a letter to bring to you."

"Just a moment," said the voice. "I am not Sir Aubrey. I am his butler, Merryweather. Sir Aubrey is in New York and will not be back for another month. I can, of course, get a message to him that you have called, and then perhaps you could call me again tomorrow after I receive his instructions. I know he did receive a letter from your father and was hoping to see you."

I hung up the phone and pondered my next move. A very attractive young lady with gorgeous golden hair, talking to two other people a few feet away, saw me looking puzzled and perhaps a little worried. She walked over and asked if I needed any help. I told her simply that I needed to find out how to get to Hollywood. "I've never met anyone in the Royal Air Force before," she said. "I'll walk you to a bus that will take you right down Sunset Boulevard into the centre of Hollywood. I'll ask the driver to drop you at a very nice servicemen's hostel I know about right on Sunset."

Ten minutes later I was on my way. Funny how some things stick in your mind. To this day I still remember her name: Opal Allen. She gave me her telephone number and suggested I call her if I ran into any difficulties. I have often wondered what happened to that delight-ful lady. After the war, I tried hard to find her when I was working in Hollywood, but I failed to make contact even though the *Los Angeles Examiner* wrote a large story about my memory. I heard from more than fifty people who had known Opal, but nobody knew where she was then living. I tried many other ways in the years ahead, but sadly, we never did again make contact.

The bus driver stopped right at the entrance of the servicemen's hostel that Opal Allen had mentioned. "It's clean and you get a great breakfast free," he said. I walked into the lobby through a crowd of American servicemen. Everyone gazed at me in my RAF uniform. At the reception desk, an elderly lady greeted me. "Royal Canadian Air Force," she said. "First we've ever had here. What brings you down from Canada?"

I explained I was not in the RCAF but the RAF, and that I was training in Canada to become a pilot. At that moment, another elderly lady came on duty. "Canadian Air Force," she said. "I'll take over, Tilly. I have something special for all Canadians visiting Hollywood." To me, she said, "I'm Ruth Henderson, what is your name?" I gave her my name and once again explained that I was not Canadian, but just training there.

"I don't think that will make any difference to Mr. and Mrs. Olcott," she said.

"Mr. and Mrs. Olcott?" I questioned.

"Sidney Olcott is Canadian," she said. "Val loves Canada too. They have instructed us to call them if any servicemen or women from Canada book in. You are the first we've had." She picked up the phone and asked for a number. Her call was answered immediately. "Val," said Ruth Henderson, "I have a Canadian flyer here. Can you come down and pick him up?" Ruth smiled at me. "Valentine—everyone calls her Val—will drive down for you," she said. "It should only take her ten minutes. The Olcotts live on Bedford Drive in Beverly Hills.

They have a beautiful home. You will be well looked after there. Now sit down and relax."

She gave me a large glass of milk and a doughnut to eat. She asked a hundred questions about England, where she said she had visited a few years before the war started. I was still trying to answer her questions when Valentine Olcott arrived. She smiled warmly spotting my uniform as she entered the lobby, rushed over and gave me a great big hug.

I must tell you, from first sight I was enchanted with Valentine Olcott. In her fifties, she radiated a beauty that is rare even in the young. I believe it came from the warmth of her heart, which she exhibited so many times during my stay in Hollywood.

"Sid and I have waited and waited for a Canadian serviceman to visit Hollywood," she said. "Now at last we have one. You will be our very special guest."

"Mrs. Olcott," I said, "I must explain that I am not Canadian; and I'm in the Royal Air Force, not the Royal Canadian Air Force. I'm just in Canada learning to fly. Then I'll be going home to England."

"What's the difference?" she asked. "RAF or RCAF—you're all so terribly brave. And my name is Valentine—but my friends call me Val—and I am sure we are going to be very good friends. My husband will be delighted when he gets home tonight to find we have you as our guest. My husband, Sidney—but you must call him Sid—was born in Canada and he loves everything about that beautiful country we have visited so often."

I thanked Mrs. Henderson, gulped down the rest of my glass of milk, picked up my kit bag and suitcase and headed out of the door with Val Olcott.

★

In 1943, Hollywood—and especially Beverly Hills—was surely the nearest thing to heaven on earth. The air was deliciously scented from masses of flowers growing everywhere and the spectacular palm trees were the first I had ever seen. The huge homes we passed were nothing less than mansions and I couldn't help wondering if some of film land's greatest stars might be just behind their giant windows.

En route to Bedford Drive in Beverly Hills, I explained what had happened to me in Canada and mentioned a few things I hoped to do in California.

"I'm sure Sid will be able to arrange anything you want," said Val. "He knows just about everyone in the motion picture industry, and though he is now retired he is well-remembered and still has many friends in high places. You have heard of the Canadian actress Mary Pickford, of course?"

"Oh yes," I replied. "Isn't she the 'Queen of Hollywood'?"

"Just about," said Val. "Mary is a good friend of ours, and any doors that need to be opened, she can open."

Sidney Olcott got home about an hour after we arrived. Val had shown me to my gorgeous bedroom with a private bathroom attached. I had showered, changed my clothes, and eaten the supper Val had prepared for me, so when Sidney arrived I felt very presentable—and hopefully a credit to the RAF—as the distinguished-looking gentlemen walked in and eyed me from head to toe. His silver hair shone as if it were polished. His blue eyes were almost piercing, but they twinkled as he spoke. His unwrinkled face had a beautiful tan and his dark grey suit looked as though it were just off the tailor's rack.

"How long can you stay with us?" was his first question.

"Well, sir," I said, "I have nineteen days' leave left, but I can't expect you to put up with me for that length of time."

"Why not?" asked Sidney. "And the name is Sid, not 'sir.' You are not in the RAF in my house."

"Of course we will be happy to have you stay right here," echoed Val.

"Our house is yours," said Sid. "If we have to go out and you are at home during mealtimes, our cook, Bessie, will make you whatever you want. I have a butler who comes in every day at ten, and if you need to go anywhere when neither Val nor I are around, he will drive you anywhere you wish. Bessie has her car too, and she will also be happy to drive you."

I felt ashamed as I tried to stifle a yawn.

"Good heavens," said Val. "You must be exhausted. When did you sleep last?"

I told her I had slept rather fitfully on the train—the first time in two days.

"Then you must go to bed right now," she said, "In the morning we can start making plans for you."

When I woke up the sun was streaming through the window. It was 10 AM. What the future held for me, I had no idea. I still really didn't even know who Sid and Val Olcott were. But I was soon to find out they were well-loved in the film industry and that Sid was still recognized as one of the most outstanding directors Hollywood had ever produced. And it was not long before one of the most important people in the film industry was showering praise on Val as an outstanding actress who had allowed her fame to be eclipsed by her husband's directorial skills.

Who that praise came from you will discover very soon.

mɛɛƬIΝG mᴀᴙY ᴘI(ᴋᴦᴏᴙᴅ:
QUɛɛΝ ᴏᴦ ᴴᴏᴸᴸYWᴏᴏᴅ

When I walked downstairs that morning, I was welcomed by both Olcotts.

"What would you like for breakfast?" asked Val.

"Could I possibly have scrambled eggs?"

"Anything you heart desires," she responded.

Before I was able to sit at the table to eat, the Olcotts were already planning my stay.

"Any first choice of something to do?" asked Sid.

"I'd love to see inside one of the studios."

"That's easy," said Sid. "Once you've eaten, we'll take a drive over to Mary Pickford's home on Summit Drive. I've already called her and she says she will be happy to see us this morning. Mary can open any door in Hollywood. After breakfast, make a list of all the people you want to meet and the places you want to see, and we'll go right over and talk to her."

It was that simple. I was reluctant to appear ignorant by asking, but I still wanted to know who the Olcotts were to have the phone numbers of people like Mary Pickford.

As it was Mary Pickford, a giant in the film industry, who made sure I understood that both Sid and Val were important people in their industry. She told me that Sid's film *From The Manger To The Cross*, which he had made in Ireland in 1912, was considered to be the greatest of all silent films. Today I own a copy of his remarkable film on tape and know why he was so admired for his work. I have to wonder what incredible things Sid would have achieved had he been able to utilize the technology available to today's directors. By 1912 Sid Olcott had made over one hundred silent films, including the first version of *Ben-Hur*, which brought him huge acclaim in 1907, and an invitation to visit the White House to be congratulated on his work in the advancement of motion pictures.

But what I failed to find out was why, since they were still only in their fifties, the Olcotts had decided to retire. Nobody could give me an answer. Obviously, living in such a beautiful home with a maid and a butler, they had plenty of money. But to leave such an industry when both were at the height of their careers didn't make sense. When I asked him why he retired at such a young age, I recall Sid saying, "My friend, there comes a time when you know you must retire. Both Val and I reached that day, and we will never work again."

The Olcott home was beautiful; but I was stunned to see Pickfair, the home of Mary Pickford, at the top of Summit Drive in Beverly Hills. It was truly magnificent: a castle for the Queen of Hollywood. Sid drove us down the open driveway and parked right by the front door. Remember, this was Beverly Hills in the 1940s. There were no gates, security guards, or high fences then. The doors of Pickfair were opened by an elderly Chinese man who graciously bowed us in. Mary and her husband, Charles "Buddy" Rogers, greeted us in the largest sitting room I had ever seen. In the centre was a huge painting of Mary much larger than the diminutive real thing, who smiled, kissed me, and gave me a great big hug.

"Welcome to my home," said Mary. "Sid has asked that I fulfill all your dreams in Hollywood and I plan to do just that. Where do you want to start?"

I told her about my letter to Sir Aubrey Smith, but explained that he was away in New York.

"I know Aubrey well. A fine gentleman," said Mary. "I will try to do all the things for you he would have done. You are staying with Sid and Val, and you couldn't get anywhere better, but if you need a break during your stay you will be welcome to stay here with Buddy and me."

"I think he'll survive nineteen days with us," said Sid. "But if by any chance you are planning one of your wonderful parties, I hope you will make sure he is invited."

Mary nodded. Seventy years later, the party she gave me is still a vivid memory that will be with me to my dying day.

"Now, Charles, I will need a list of all the things you want to do," said Mary.

I handed over the list I had hastily made up at the Olcotts'. It contained about a dozen items.

"Is this all?" she asked. "I think I would like to add a few more ideas of my own. But where do you want to start? What can I do right now so you won't waste a minute?"

"I'm not sure I can take more excitement in one day than I have already had in meeting you and Buddy," I said. "I always imagined Pickfair was only open to celebrities."

"You are a celebrity," said Mary. "In this town, real people are hard to find. You are a real person and therefore a celebrity. Buddy and I are honoured to have you in our home. We hope you will visit often while you are in Hollywood. But let's start making plans. What do you want to see first?"

I'd like to visit one of the studios," I said. "Can you get me inside one of them? Dare I suggest Metro-Goldwyn-Mayer?"

"One?" said Mary. "All of them, if you want. But MGM, certainly. Are you aware that Louis Mayer, the man who runs that great studio, is Canadian?"

"No," I said. "Is this city populated by Canadians?"

"We like to think it was built by Canadians," said Mary. Without another word, she picked up a telephone and asked the operator for a number. "Mr. Mayer, please," she said. "Mary Pickford calling." Seconds later, she continued: "Louie, Mary here. I have a surprise for you. I have a Canadian airman visiting me and he wants to visit your studio. When can he come over?" There was a pause. "Excellent, Louie. Then we shall give him lunch here and I shall have him driven over to you. Shall we say he will be on your doorstep at one o'clock?"

Another pause. Mary smiled. "Perfect."

She put down the phone and spoke to me. "Everything is arranged. Louie is getting his afternoon free so he can show you his studio. You'll like him. He's a very ordinary man, but very important. Used to work in his father's scrap metal yard in Saint John—that's in New Brunswick. Have you been to New Brunswick?" When I told her my first stop in Canada had been Moncton and that I had visited Saint John to see the Reversing Falls, she was delighted. "Be sure you tell Louie that you were in his hometown. He talks about Canada often. It is very important to him," she said. "Today I think you will find you are very important, too, at MGM."

Half an hour later I was on my way, after promising Mary to keep one evening open for the party she planned to give for me. "I want a list of everyone you want to meet. They'll be here," she said. "In Hollywood, nobody turns my invitations down." A week later, I found that to be true.

LOUIS B. MAYER NEVER
FORGOT SAINT JOHN

When I first prepared to meet Louis B. Mayer in 1943 at Metro-Goldwyn-Mayer Studios in Hollywood, I was almost trembling in my shoes. Mary Pickford had been so down-to-earth that it was impossible to think of her as anything more than the girl next door—if you forgot the fact that she was probably worth more millions than anyone else I was ever likely to meet. But Louis B. Mayer was different.

I had heard and read stories about Mayer. The movie magazines suggested he was tough, mean, difficult, abrupt, inconsiderate—even selfish. I imagined that immediately after we'd met he would probably hand me over to some underling, who would take me around and let me see a few of the sets in the gigantic studio. But just getting inside MGM was great. If that was the way it was going to be, I was still delighted to see what the day would bring.

I was totally unprepared when a rather small, slightly overweight man came running down the steps of the administration building at MGM Studios to greet me. That it was the great Louis B. Mayer, there was no doubt. His image had been printed in a million newspapers and magazines for many years.

"My friend from Canada," he yelled as Mary's car came to a stop near the foot of the steps. "Welcome to my studio. I am so happy to greet a fellow Canadian. Hopefully I can make today a day you will never forget." He put out his hand and shook mine until it nearly came off. "An RAF man," he said. "We don't see many of you down here, but we are very proud of you. Very proud. Let's go to my office, where we can discuss my plans for you. Anything you don't like, we shall change. The rest of this day is yours, my friend. Everything in my studio is at your command."

The six hours that followed I shall never forget. Mayer certainly did not hand me over to an underling. He spent until almost seven that night escorting me personally into every nook and cranny of the huge MGM Studios. Everywhere we went, he made a point of telling people I was his Canadian guest. He introduced me to so many stars I lost count, and I quickly realized that I was, for some startling reason, being treated like a VIP. I especially recall meeting Ronald Colman, Cary Grant, June Allyson, Jimmy Durante, Donald Meek, Edward Arnold, Esther Williams, Kathryn Grayson, Van Johnson, Gene Kelly, George Murphy, Katherine Hepburn, Basil Rathbone, Robert Young, Mickey Rooney, Dick Powell, Alan and Sue Carol Ladd, Gloria DeHaven, Lewis Stone, Herbert Marshall, and Jean Porter. (Never heard of Jean Porter? You should find her photo on the Internet. I dreamed about her for weeks. I could go on forever....)

Mayer explained my unexpected status very simply. "I'm Canadian," he said. "You are here from Canada. I love Canada. It was Saint John, New Brunswick, that gave my parents sanctuary, a home, and a chance to succeed in life, and taught me to understand that if you work hard, anything in the world is possible."

He talked incessantly about his work on the dockyard in Saint John, how he had often worked twelve or more hours a day picking up scrap metal and other recyclable items for his father's scrap yard. "I still work those same hours today at MGM," he said. "I want you to know that I despise any man or woman who says eight hours of work is enough. Enough only comes when the work you have to do is complete. I learned that in New Brunswick. They know how to work up there. I have more than thirty people from New Brunswick working in my studio. I don't ever have to tell them to get their jobs completed."

This proud Canadian destroyed every bad word I had heard about him during the six hours I was in his studio. It was obvious that the many stars I met loved him. Many told me clearly that without Mayer they would never have achieved fame and success. He knew the name of every worker in the studio. I recall him asking one man who was sweeping a set if his wife was now feeling better. "Thanks to you providing the medical help she needed L. B.," he replied, "she is now well on the way to recovery."

When my incredible day was over, I was not sent home in a studio car. I sat in the back of Louis B. Mayer's own car, with Mayer beside me, as his chauffeur drove us back to the home of Sidney Olcott where I was so fortunate to be staying. His final words as I got out of the car were these: "If you can convince Sid Olcott to direct just one film at my studio, I will give you ten thousand dollars. Ask him!"

Over supper, I did ask Sid. "Sorry," he said, "I'm retired. L. B. knows that. Nothing will ever change my mind." And nothing ever did. Sid Olcott never directed again, for reasons we shall never know. In fact, he never again set foot in any one of Hollywood's film studios.

Could anything top my day at MGM? I doubted it until the phone rang at around ten o'clock that night. Sid handed over the phone. "It's L. B. for you," he said.

"I will have my car pick you up at eleven-thirty in the morning," said Mayer. "There isn't much traffic and you should be here in less than fifteen minutes. I have a little surprise for you. Everything is arranged. Will that time be acceptable to you?" Of course it was acceptable. "Yes, please," I said. I couldn't imagine what the surprise might be, but I was more than ready to accept anything he might have planned.

★

At ten minutes before noon next day, I walked up the steps to the administration building at MGM once more. Mayer was standing at the top, rubbing his hands together as though he had achieved something very special. I couldn't begin to imagine what the surprise might possibly be.

He led me into his private study. "I like you," he said. "You have a nice attitude. I think you should consider making our city your home. If you approve, I can get you a medical certificate saying you are not healthy enough to continue with your military service and you can stay right here from today on if you wish. I will put you on my payroll and you can be trained in any aspect of this great industry you choose. What do you say? But I must tell you, with those two front teeth of yours, I don't think we can ever make you photogenic enough to become an actor!"

I was stunned. Yes, I must admit, I was even tempted by this astonishing offer. What had I done to deserve this? But there was a war on in England. My family was in middle of it. "Mr. Mayer," I said, "such an offer is unbelievable to me. But I joined the RAF to become a pilot, and until the end of this war, I cannot think of coming here to live. We have a war to win."

Mayer slapped me on the back. "You have courage," he said. "But my offer stands after the war. Come back here and I will make all your dreams come true. Now come with me. I want to show you what we Canadians think of our old country."

Fifteen minutes later, I discovered that he was not by any means the only Canadian in Hollywood proud of his country of birth. Mayer and I walked into a private room leading from the studio commissary (that's the restaurant at MGM), and there I saw a long table set out for twelve people.

"This will be a moment I believe you will never forget," said Mayer. "You are at the head of the table. I will be in this chair at the other end. Now sit down while I bring in your special guests." As soon as I was seated, the door opened. Mayer, still standing, announced each visitor individually. "Your first guest," he said, "is Walter Pidgeon from my hometown, Saint John, New Brunswick." Walter Pidgeon walked down to me, shook my hand, and said a few words before taking the top seat on the right side of the long table.

The introductions continued. The names were those of some of the most renowned stars in Hollywood. To my amazement, I found they were all from Canada: Fay Wray from Cardston, Alberta; Jack Carson from Carmen, Manitoba; Ann Rutherford from Vancouver, British Columbia; Cecilia Parker from Fort William, Ontario; Deanna Durbin from Winnipeg, Manitoba; Rod Cameron from Calgary, Alberta;

Fifi D'Orsay from Montreal, Quebec; Walter Huston from Toronto, Ontario; and Jack Warner from London, Ontario. My renowned guests chatted with me across the table or walked over to stand beside me and talk mostly about Canada. It was obvious that although they were stars in Hollywood, Canada was still very important to them. I hope Mayer understood why I didn't eat any of my lunch on that momentous day. Louis B. Mayer's all-Canadian luncheon will always be the most astonishing memory of my life. At twenty years old, I was being honoured in an unbelievable way.

After the luncheon ended, these great stars of Hollywood did not rush away to their studios and homes. They stayed with me for over three hours, and each one was obviously genuinely concerned about the war going on in Europe. Would you believe that no fewer than seven of these stars wrote to my parents in England to say I was recovering well from my illness and would soon be home again?

Jack Warner—who told me this occasion was the first time in ten years he had sat down with Mayer without arguing—invited me to his studio to meet his stars. (That visit I shall tell you about in a while.)

Deanna Durbin invited me to dinner with her family, who she said were from Manchester, near my home in England, and wanted to talk to me. Deanna's father promised to write to my parents and say I was looking well after my illness. (He kept his word, as my father showed me proudly, along with the other stars' letters, when I returned home after getting my wings.)

A few days later, I visited Walter Pidgeon at his beautiful home and began a friendship that lasted until the day he died.

All the others gave me phone numbers and told me to call them if I needed any help making my vacation memorable. I spoke to all of them later and visited five where they were filming.

All but one of these giants have now left this earth, but I remained in touch with all of them for many years. I met the last survivor of that wonderful day again a few years ago, in the beautiful home just outside Paris, France, to which she had retired. Deanna Durbin smiled as she recalled the luncheon. "I had never liked Louie Mayer until that day," she said. "But what he did showed that we were all Canadians at heart and I loved him for that." I am still in touch with her, and almost had her convinced to spend a month in Canada in 2010. She was to stay with us for a week before visiting her hometown, Winnipeg. Two weeks before the visit she phoned to say she had been very ill and, with great regret, had to cancel her travel plans.

That a man like Louis Mayer, so important and successful in the Hollywood film industry, would go to the trouble to organize a luncheon for a totally unimportant RAF pilot trainee still bewilders me seventy years later. But that sort of thing is what made Hollywood in its golden years so great and totally unforgettable.

When I returned to Hollywood to work after the war, I visited each of the ten luncheon stars in their homes to let them know I would never forget their kindness during the war. At the home of the Canadian-born star Fay Wray, I couldn't help admiring several beautiful ceramic creations hanging on the walls. "Where on earth do you find such wonderful things?" I asked. "Find them? I make them," she said. "Ceramics are my hobby. It gives me peace of mind in this uncertain world."

As I was about to leave, she asked which of her gorgeous creations I liked most. I pointed to one that was unique. It had a superbly designed plate embossed with a stork and from the plate hung six equally cleverly created platelets. She walked over to the wall, lifted it off its hanger and handed it to me. "It is yours," she said. "Thank you for helping bring peace to this world. And if this souvenir helps you remember me, I shall be very happy."

To this day, the beautiful ceramic made by Fay Wray hangs in a place of honour in the hallway of my home in Riverview, New Brunswick. Many people have admired it over the years, but sadly, when I say, "It was made by Fay Wray," the younger visitors almost always say, "Fay who?" But I don't believe any real film buff will ever forget this delectable heroine of one of the greatest films still known today: *King Kong*.

ONLY CHARLIE CHAPLIN COULD HAVE
GOTTEN ME INTO HEARST CASTLE

Charlie Chaplin, a great admirer of Sid Olcott's directorial abilities, dropped in to Sid and Val's home on the third evening of my visit. When he heard of the luncheon given me by Louis B. Mayer—a man he obviously disliked intensely, for some reason he would never explain—he was infuriated. "I will do something much better than that to make your visit to Hollywood memorable," Charlie said before he left the house.

What that "something" was to be, none of us had any idea. Sid and Val were a little concerned because Charlie was rather notorious for his wild parties, and many of the young girls he invited to these sessions were not exactly the most "angelic" in the film industry. So they warned him that whatever he planned to do had to be in good taste or I wouldn't be allowed to be there.

Charlie called a few days later to say he planned to take me somewhere nobody else in Hollywood could, and that his surprise would be far more impressive than Louie Mayer's luncheon. He asked that I pack my bag for a two-day trip. But he would provide no more information. We discussed his failure to say where he was taking me and I, with some reluctance, agreed with Sid and Val that unless he provided more details, I would not be going. When he arrived at the Olcotts's front door to pick me up on the first Friday of my stay, Sid and Val made it clear to Charlie that I would be going nowhere until they were sure it was a safe place for me to visit, and that there would be no regrets or repercussions from the trip.

Finally, when it was obvious that Sid and Val wouldn't let me out of the house until he divulged his secret, Charlie Chaplin started to talk.

"I am taking him where only I can take him," he said. "We have been invited by William Randolph Hearst to be his guests at San Simeon and Charles is to be the guest of honour this weekend. Hearst's plane is waiting for us now at the Burbank airport. Is that acceptable?"

Today the doors of the late William Randolph Hearst's renowned castle (popularly known as *La Cuesta Encantada*, in San Simeon, in the hills of northern California), are open to anyone willing to pay the sizeable admission fee. But during the Second World War, the only people who visited this amazing castle were those invited by Mr. Hearst himself. Of course, such a journey was completely acceptable. Sid Olcott agreed with Chaplin that the invitation he had secured for me to visit Hearst's Castle as a VIP weekend guest was the ultimate achievement.

Chaplin's chauffeur drove us to a small airport in Burbank. Both of us took nothing more than overnight bags. I had bought some civilian clothes in Hollywood but nobody seemed to want me to wear them. Chaplin insisted that I go to San Simeon in my RAF uniform. "Mr. Hearst has demanded it," he said. We flew from Burbank to San Simeon in Hearst's private plane, which was waiting for the two of us.

We landed on Hearst's private landing strip in San Simeon. There we were met by a limousine that took us up a winding road to the amazing castle standing at the top of the enchanted hill. Four luxurious bungalows stood on the grounds of the castle. Each bungalow had two separate suites containing a bedroom, bathroom, and sitting room. Chaplin was taken to one suite, while I was shown to the other in the same building. Hearst's secretary, who had met us, told me that if there was anything I wanted I simply had to pick up the phone by the bed and my request would be attended to immediately.

Chaplin called a few minutes after my arrival. "Want to see the castle?" he asked. "I've been here quite a few times and know every square inch of the place." The two of us went on surely the most fascinating tour I have ever been fortunate enough to take in my entire life.

The huge dining room in the castle had one long table large enough to seat fifty guests. The great hall was hung with the banners of British knights, and suits of armour stood majestically every six feet. The vast library contained nothing but leather-bound volumes. Hearst himself told me later there were five thousand books. "I've read every one," he said proudly.

We looked into each of the richly furnished guest rooms in the castle. None were yet occupied. They were the most beautiful rooms I have ever seen. "Many of the paintings on the walls are worth $250,000," said Chaplin. "The rooms will all be full later. Hearst's other guests are coming up with him from Los Angeles on his private train. You'll meet people here you would likely never get a chance to meet anywhere else."

If there were guards or any security systems in the castle, I never saw them. Everything was open to us. No doors were locked. We went through the entire castle—except for the third floor. "That's where Hearst lives," said Chaplin. "He and his actress friend, Marion Davies, occupy the entire floor. Hearst's wife has her own home in Beverly Hills. The castle is reserved for Hearst and Marion."

After an hour examining the splendours of the castle, Chaplin and I walked the grounds. Most impressive was a Roman swimming pool surrounded by huge marble statues imported from Europe. At the pool, a member of the house staff approached us. "Would you like your lunch served by the pool, in your suites, or in the main dining hall?" he asked. Chaplin answered with a grin: "In the dining hall, please." To me, he added, "You are going to see something unique there, I promise."

I did indeed. In this magnificent dining room, where the china was exquisite and the cutlery solid silver, the entire scene was made to look odd—apparently at the insistence of Hearst, large bottles of tomato sauce bearing their store labels were placed everywhere along the table. "Maybe he owns the company," said Chaplin. "I don't have a clue."

Hearst was not scheduled to arrive until late in the afternoon, along with his other weekend guests, so we were told to swim or just relax by the pool and enjoy the scenery until they arrived. The "scenery" included more wild animals than I had ever seen in a zoo. Giraffes, camels, kangaroos, zebras, and even an elephant walked up to within a few feet of where we stood. They were part of Hearst's exotic "farm." All of them were completely tame, as I discovered when I walked over to them. They were obviously being well treated.

"There will be seven other guests with Mr. Hearst. Miss Davies will not be here this weekend. A list of all the other guests will be delivered to you in about an hour," said the secretary. If Charlie knew who else was to be there, he didn't reveal the secret; it was to be a wonderful surprise.

GRETA GARBO CERTAINLY
DIDN'T WANT TO BE ALONE

That I was a guest at William Randolph Hearst's famous castle atop the enchanted hill was something that still felt like a dream, when Mr. Hearst's secretary walked up to Chaplin and me sitting by the pool and handed a copy of Mr. Hearst's weekend guest list to each of us. I was certainly not a Very Important Person. But at the top of the list was my own name and beneath it these words: *Charles Foster, representing the British Royal Air Force, will be my guest of honour this weekend.* The other guests followed in alphabetical order: Mr. Charles Chaplin, Mr. W. C. Fields, Miss Greta Garbo, Mr. Howard Hughes, Mr. Charles Lederer, Mr. Charles Lindbergh, and Mr. and Mrs. Herman Mankiewicz.

"This is your weekend," said Chaplin. "Who would you like to sit next to at dinner tonight? Mr. Hearst will, of course, be at the head of the table. You will be in the first seat to his right. Now who do you want sitting next to you?"

"As a future pilot, I suppose I should say Howard Hughes or Charles Lindbergh, but, wow, can I please sit next to Greta Garbo?"

"You certainly can," said Chaplin. "I will arrange it."

When the guests arrived in three limousines from the railway station near San Simeon, I watched with a little awe.

"Greet your host first," said Chaplin. "W. R." he said. "I would like to introduce you to your guest of honour, Mr. Charles Foster."

Hearst shook my hand with a firm grip. "I am honoured to have you here, Charles," he said. "The British Royal Air Force is a credit to the world. My home is yours this weekend. Now, may I introduce you to my other guests?"

I shook hands with Howard Hughes, Charles Lindbergh, Herman and Dorothy Mankiewicz, W. C. Fields, and Charles Lederer. Only one remained. Garbo stepped forward, ignoring my outstretched hand, put her arms around me, hugged me tight, and then gave me a kiss on the lips that had me shivering in my shoes.

"I adore the RAF," she said. I remember to this day looking into those gorgeous eyes and wondering when I would wake up from my dream. Greta Garbo, reputed to be the Hollywood star who spoke little and always "wanted to be alone," did not live up to her reputation on that wonderful weekend.

Dinner, which was served in Hearst's private dining room on the third floor, was at an intimate table that seated just the ten of us. Greta Garbo and I talked so much I don't think I ate. I turned to Mr. Hearst and apologized.

"Charles," he said, "if I were sitting where you are, I too would talk to Greta. We can talk later. But do eat your dinner, I assure you it is delicious."

Garbo and I talked about the war and the bombs on London. She obviously read newspapers thoroughly. She asked if I had a special girl back in England. When I said no, she said, "Good, then I will be your special girl until this awful war is over."

She asked if I knew who all the other guests were.

"Mr. Lindbergh and Mr. Hughes are renowned fliers," I said. "Mr. Chaplin got me this invitation, you I never dreamed I would meet and talk with, Mr. Mankiewicz I am told by Mr. Chaplin is a screenwriter— could his wife be an actress?"

"Wife?" said Garbo with a wicked laugh. "That girl may be an actress, but she is certainly not his wife."

"W. C. Fields I have laughed at for years. I hope to talk with him later. Mr. Lederer, too, I know as a writer. He was pointed out to me at MGM when I was there."

"Charles Lederer is not here not because he is a writer," said Garbo, "He is here because his mother is the sister of Marion Davies, our host's mistress, who unfortunately you will not meet this weekend."

I played tennis with Greta Garbo the next morning. I only won because she let me. We talked for hours, and seemed to have a rapport that one only dreams about having with a person as famous and dazzling as Garbo. We sat together at lunch and dinner, and I can still recall vividly the three additional kisses she gave me for some reason or other throughout the weekend. (I only wished there could have been thirty more reasons!)

Garbo loved swimming, but since I couldn't swim I had a chance to talk with Mr. Hearst and W. C. Fields. Fields showed me how he got around the very strict "no liquor" policy at the castle. He unscrewed the top of his walking stick and took a long drink of what he proudly described as Hearst's "forbidden fruit." I have often wondered if Hearst knew about Fields's illegal liquor store. Since by day two the great comedian was not walking any too steadily, I have to believe Hearst, like me, enjoyed Fields's carefree attitude towards life and decided that it was more important than official castle rules.

I saw Greta Garbo twice more before my stay in Hollywood ended. Once we joined Charlie Chaplin and actress Sheila Ryan for a game of tennis, and later the two of us shared a private dinner in her home—a meal that she herself had cooked. All I remember of that dinner was Garbo's parting comment as her chauffeur was about to drive me back to Sid Olcott's home: "Charles," she said, "you didn't eat much. Was my cooking so bad?"

"Oh no," I said, "it was wonderful." Looking her straight in the eyes, I added, "But you were so very much better." Again she kissed me.

We wrote more than a dozen letters back and forth over the next ten years, but I wouldn't see her again until 1989, in New York City. Garbo, by then a recluse, had allowed nobody other than staff into her New York brownstone for many years. Writers who had spent nights outside her door begging to be given an interview had all been ignored. Some of the most persistent had even been arrested. Astonishingly, she opened her doors to me. It was a day I will remember until I leave this earth.

HERMAN MANKIEWICZ TOLD ME
A REMARKABLE SECRET

When I went to bed the first night in the luxurious bungalow provided for me on the castle grounds, it was still beyond belief to me that, thanks to Charlie Chaplin, I was not only a visitor but officially guest of honour at William Randolph Heart's amazing castle.

That Charlie Chaplin, who was probably at that time the most important man in Hollywood, had arranged my visit and was in the second suite in the same bungalow as me was also amazing.

That Greta Garbo, reputed to be a near recluse, had kissed me and spent hours talking to me would have been unimaginable twenty-four hours earlier.

That I had met Charles Lindbergh, the first man to fly across the Atlantic, and shared a coffee with millionaire aviator and filmmaker Howard Hughes, were two more events that had me wondering if I had simply been dreaming this entire incredible weekend.

That I had been greeted by William Randolph Hearst as if I was somebody important, and had enjoyed a laugh with W. C. Fields, one of the comedic giants of Hollywood, are moments I can still see clearly seven decades later, if I close my eyes and dream a little.

I had seen very little of Herman Mankiewicz, who was fully occupied trying to enhance his future with the lady he had called his "wife;" but it was he who, despite my enchantment with Garbo, left me with one of the most satisfying memories of my entire life. With one remarkable story, Herman Mankiewicz changed my entire outlook on my father, who was then thousands of kilometres away in war-torn England.

★

Chaplin was puzzled that Mankiewicz was there at all. Just two years earlier, as he pointed out, Mankiewicz had scripted the film *Citizen Kane*, starring Orson Welles. Hearst had tried to buy and destroy the film because he considered it a slanderous attack on his own fascinating, but somewhat infamous, life. Neither Chaplin nor myself ever found out why Mankiewicz, whose name was not allowed to be printed anywhere in the entire Hearst newspaper and magazine empire, was there at all. When I asked Mr. Hearst, he replied simply, with a broad grin, "When you get as old as me, you will discover there are some things it is better not to know." I have in my own aging years certainly discovered the wisdom of that statement.

When Herman Mankiewicz approached me by the Roman pool and suggested we go for a walk around the castle grounds, I was intrigued enough to accept.

"Your father was Charles Foster, a British army captain in the First World War, was he not?" Mankiewicz asked as we started the walk.

"Yes." I said, startled at his comment. "How on earth did you know that?"

"Your name, and the fact that you look so much like he looked when we met in Paris in 1919, gave me no doubt who you were from the moment we were introduced," replied Mankiewicz. "In 1919 I was working for the *Chicago Tribune*, based in Paris, France," he said. "One night, walking back to my hotel, I was accosted by a number of the many homeless louts who wandered the Paris streets at night. One produced a knife and demanded my money. When I refused, they started hitting me and I was thrown on the ground. They then started kicking me. Suddenly a man in a British military uniform ran across the street and started punching my assailants. It was a remarkable act of heroism. There were perhaps six or more of them to the two of us. But they ran away and the British captain picked me up off the sidewalk. He helped me back to my hotel and we shared a glass of wine before he had to leave.

"That man, Charles, was your father, Charles Foster. He saved me from a terrible beating—possibly even saved my life, for those ruffians had no respect for the living. Your father was leaving for London the next day and we never did meet again. But I gave him a promise that night that one day I would put his name in the world's history books for his courage. I had no idea at that time how I was going to do that.

"By 1930 I was back in New York working as a drama critic for the *New York Times*. One of my friends was Broadway and radio actor Orson Welles. In 1939 he approached me with the outline of a story he wanted made into a screenplay. In 1940 I started writing the script and moved to Los Angeles with Welles. The film, released in Hollywood in 1941, was *Citizen Kane*, loosely based on the far-from-respectable life of our host here today, William Randolph Hearst."

"Then why—" I started to ask, but my question was interrupted by Mankiewicz.

"You want to know why I am here with Hearst, but what I am about to tell you is much more important. It is a story that I have never told anyone but your father before today. I finally conceived a way to enshrine your father's name forever through the medium of the motion picture industry. I decided to call my reincarnation of Mr. Hearst, Charles Foster Kane. I threatened to quit the project if Welles would not agree to the name, and he knew that if I abandoned the script the film would never be made. I wrote and told your father what I was doing, but he never replied. That was our last communication, but I always hoped he did know what I had done."

I said my father had never mentioned the incident in Paris, nor the fact that his name was immortalized in *Citizen Kane*. But I promised to immediately ask if he had ever received the letter about the use of his name when I returned to England. I pointed out that a bomb had destroyed our home in 1941, and that mail at that time might well never have reached my father.

"The screenplay for *Citizen Kane* won the Oscar and I actually planned to send the trophy to your father, but Welles, who had written almost nothing of the script, claimed the Oscar with me and I never saw it again after that night. To this day, Welles still has it but has never offered to share it with me. He and I no longer talk." (It should be put on record that Orson Welles, after the death of Herman Mankiewicz in 1953, took the Oscar to Mankiewicz's widow, saying, "This should have been Herman's. Please take it.")

I was so silent when I returned to my chair by the pool that both Chaplin and Garbo asked me what was wrong. It was only then that I realized the importance of the Mankiewicz story. I smiled. "Wrong? Nothing," I said. "I have just learned to see my father in a very different and wonderful light."

I was still visualizing the rather pompous, baldheaded, somewhat overweight father I had known until that time. I had never thought of him as a hero. Shame on me.

I did ask my father about Herman Mankiewicz on my first visit home to England after I had graduated and earned my wings. "Yes, I did hear from Herman," he said, "but we were and still are in a war. I didn't have time to think that such a gesture was important. Is it really so important now?"

And to the day he died, that was all he would say about the honour.

CHARLES LINDBERGH
ASKED ME TO BE HIS PILOT

Charles Lindbergh and Howard Hughes generously noticed I was quite content being enchanted by Garbo, so I saw little of them during the weekend at the castle. I know they spent long periods of time in deep conversation with Mr. Hearst and I have often wondered if anything memorable came from those discussions. They seemed so engrossed in their talks that I had to hope they were at least trying to solve some of the world's problems, including the Second World War. But they did take time out to tell me they would be flying back to Los Angeles with Chaplin and me. "We'll have a few hours to talk then," said Lindbergh. Charles Lederer was the only disappointment. He seemed to have little interest in talking about anything. He was too busy pandering to Randolph Hearst.

At the Hearst landing-strip airport at the foot of the enchanted hill I was astonished to learn that I was to fly the plane back to the Burbank airport. I told them I had never flown a plane this powerful in Calgary or Bowden and really didn't have enough experience to tackle the takeoff. But both Lindbergh and Hughes insisted I prove to them that I had the ability to become a pilot.

Somehow, with Charles Lindbergh sitting in the second pilot's seat, prepared to take over if necessary, I got the plane into the air, to the chosen height of ten thousand feet, and on course to our destination, without him having to touch the controls. Somehow I kept the flight straight and level, despite having many animated conversations about flying with both Lindbergh and Hughes. Of the many times I met and later worked with Charlie Chaplin, I have never again heard him keep his mouth closed for such a length of time. He just smiled and listened.

As we approached Burbank, I suggested to Lindbergh that it would be safer if he took over and made the landing. Happily, he didn't argue and took over the controls—a decision that probably averted a front-page story and made certain we were all alive at the end of the day.

But this incredible pilot was a kind man. "You'll make a fine pilot," said Lindbergh. "I think you could have made the landing and will make many good ones even more difficult than this in the years ahead."

"If you want a job after the war is over, come and see me. I'll have a job for you," said Hughes. Sadly, I never saw the great flyer again.

The next time I saw Charles Lindbergh was in Niagara Falls, Ontario, long after the war was over. This famous man actually remembered me. And he gave me an interview when he had earlier that day refused to speak with major national newspaper writers covering his visit. Since I was then a reporter for the *Niagara Falls Evening Review*, a quite small daily, we had the privilege of a front-page scoop the next morning.

THANKS TO JACK WARNER,
I MADE A FRIEND FOR LIFE

By the time Jack Warner called me at Sid Olcott's, as he had promised during Louie Mayer's luncheon, Sid had given me a lot of information about him and his renowned Warner Brothers Studio.

Jack was—as were the vast majority of the studio heads in Hollywood—Jewish, and as such, hated what Germany was doing to the world and to the Jewish people at that time. I was told that Warner and his biggest star, Errol Flynn, hated each other intensely. There was a major rumor going around Hollywood at the time that Flynn might be a supporter of Germany because of his hated of Jewish people.

"Be careful of anything you say about your training or the RAF to Flynn if you meet him," said Sid. "Who knows where the information he gets is going."

Sid drove me to the Warner Studio in Burbank, but, as usual, refused to go in through the gates. I was welcomed by the security guard, who was obviously expecting me, and a secretary took me to Jack Warner's office.

Warner, like Louis B. Mayer, showed me a kindness that I, as a mere trainee pilot, certainly didn't deserve. He personally took me around the studio and introduced me to every star on the lot. I was delighted to see that this supposedly aloof man knew the name of every person in his huge studio. Like Mayer, he greeted cleaners and stars alike, asking about family members. I recall one occasion when he offered a studio technician his personal car and driver so he could go to the hospital to see his wife, who had been in a car accident.

But the studio's biggest star—the great Errol Flynn—did not appear. In view of what I had been told, I didn't want to ask too many questions, but was told by a cameraman that he didn't come to the studio unless he was actually working, and he was not scheduled that day. "He and Warner don't see eye to eye on many things," he said, "They feud like dogs and cats." I was disappointed I would not meet Flynn, then one of the greatest stars in the film industry, but didn't dare raise the problem with the very helpful and friendly Jack Warner, who had gone out of his way to be the perfect host.

When we returned to Warner's office just before lunch, I heard a voice inside from someone talking to one of the secretaries. It was undoubtedly the very distinguished and easily recognizable voice of the renowned Errol Flynn. I feared my wonderful day was to end in the middle of a Flynn-Warner battle. What could he possibly be doing inside the inner sanctum of the man he hated? This was another occasion when I discovered there are often two sides to every story, a lesson I have since remembered and taken into consideration throughout my life.

As Warner opened his office door, the unmistakable Errol Flynn rushed over and gave him a giant and very warm hug. The smile of delight on Warner's face told me instantly there something very wrong with the stories I had been told. Within minutes, it was obvious that Flynn and Warner were certainly not enemies, not feuding, but were the greatest of friends.

"I kept Errol until lunch," said Warner, "because he and I have something very important we want to discuss with you. We shall have our lunch in the office while we talk over what we hope you will agree to do to help bring a speedy end to this awful war in Europe. We need you to help trap a German spy." That was the day Errol Flynn first called me "Sport"—the only name he ever called me throughout our long and happy friendship, which lasted until the day he died.

I quickly learned from Errol and Jack that they wanted to trap a German actor, Peter Van Eyck, then working in Hollywood, into revealing his involvement as a German spy. I had met Peter while visiting actress Sheila Ryan at 20th Century Fox studios and had actually taken a photo of him with my Kodak box camera as he left the studio in his car. He had given me no indication that he might be in favour of Germany. In fact, to this day I remember him as a very pleasant person. But it was obvious that Errol and Jack knew differently. I discovered the "Flynn hates Warner" rumour had been started to see if Van Eyck would slip up and reveal his ambitions. (It was true. He had actually approached Errol to help Germany win the war.)

Errol, with Warner (who were, along with Louis Mayer, two of Hollywood's many renowned Jewish personalities) gave the project his full blessing and co-operation, and agreed he would do whatever necessary to defeat the Nazis. Van Eyck told Errol that Germany desperately wanted to discover the secret of the Norden bombsight, an invention of former Dutch engineer Carl Norden, who had immigrated to the US in 1904. Norden's latest version of the bombsight contained a mechanical computer, which allowed pilots to drop bombs from amazing heights with pinpoint accuracy. It was causing devastation in Germany, where it had already aided in the total destruction of major ammunition sites.

"Can you get inside the Norden plant?" Van Eyck asked Errol. The production plant was in southern California, not far from Hollywood. "We want pictures of the bombsight being made."

"And that, Sport," said Errol to me, "is where you come in!" He explained that with the co-operation of the United States military—who obviously knew the secret of the phony talks between Flynn and Van Eyck—I would be used as the reason why Flynn would drive to the plant.

"Van Eyck has already given me a unique mini-camera," he said. "We are to use this to get pictures of the bombsight being built."

"I can't be part of anything like that," I said. "And why do you need me?"

"Because as a member of the RAF, the Norden people will welcome you into their plant and Van Eyck will have no suspicion that we are planning to double-cross him."

"Double-cross! How?" I asked.

"The US military will set everything up," said Errol. "Van Eyck's camera will stay here at the studio, and Jack and his model-makers will build, without having any knowledge of the real bombsight, a fake that they will take pictures of. We won't have any camera at the Norden plant. All we will do is see the plant, and certainly not learn any secrets. But Van Eyck will hear that we are going and I think we can fool the bastard completely."

Of course, I was thrilled to be asked to be part of such a venture, which was already scheduled for two days ahead. And obviously Warner and Flynn had no doubt I would go along with their plan.

The Lukas-Harold Company, builders of the Norden, sent a car to take Errol and me to the plant. There, we were greeted by Carl Norden himself. He was obviously in on the plot to trap Van Eyck, because he chatted about the clever plan quite openly to Errol and me. When I walked into the production plant wearing my RAF uniform the entire staff stopped working and applauded me. It was a memorable day. In addition to feeling that I was actually helping bring the war a little closer to an end, I met a man who remained a close friend. Errol Flynn, despite all the stories you may have read about his womanizing and drinking, became one of the few people in this world I would trust with my life.

When we returned to Warner's in Carl Norden's personal car, we discovered that what the studio model-makers had produced was nothing like the bombsight we had seen, but looked extremely believable. All this was captured on the mini-camera, and the final touch was to photograph some documents that Carl Norden gave us: they had been cleverly made up at the plant and didn't mean a darn thing. As Carl said, "They will keep the Germans puzzling for months trying to figure out what on earth they mean."

The next day, Flynn handed over the camera to Peter Van Eyck. I never did find out what happened to Van Eyck, but Sheila Ryan, in a letter she sent me in Canada after I returned to my training, told me he had been quietly ushered out of 20th Century Fox Studios one day by the US Army and had not returned.

But I did see him again after the war in 1956.

I was then working on the *Errol Flynn Theatre* television series in London, England, and Errol had been invited to the Berlin International Film Festival. He asked me to go along with him. At the official reception, we were a little shocked to see a much plumper but still recognizable Peter Van Eyck. He was obviously there in some official capacity as a member of the festival organization. Suddenly he spotted Flynn. I could see a snarl on his face as he ran across the room and took a wild swing at Errol. "You bastard," he said. Those were his final words that day. Van Eyck's swing missed, but Errol's didn't, and seconds later Van Eyck was flat on his back on the ground. The German spy was out cold. Security men picked him up and carried him out of the room.

Later, we learned that Van Eyck had returned to the US after providing the American army with some vital information. He did resume his acting career in Hollywood, but he died at age fifty-seven in 1969. For the rest of his life, Errol was convinced Van Eyck was murdered and that he knew who was responsible. "Good riddance," was all he would say.

BUT EVERYTHING WONDERFUL
MUST FINALLY END

It would take a second book to tell you about all the other things that happened to me in Hollywood all those years ago. But hopefully I have not ignored the kindness of those who deserve special recognition.

There were so many Canadians in Hollywood—all important people—and Sid and Val Olcott made quite sure I met as many of them as possible. Meeting the Canadians meant I met the other people working with them, and at the end of my visit my autograph book was full of the biggest names in Hollywood. One of these proud Canadians was Sam De Grasse, who was once known as the "most evil man in Hollywood" because of his fine acting roles in the silent era. Even though he had left Bathurst, New Brunswick, when he was only nine years old, he remembered the name of the teacher there, John Kingsley, who had told him one day he would become an actor.

In 1943 it was Ontario-born Allan Dwan, then directing Dennis O'Keefe and William Bendix in *Abroad With Two Yanks*, who made me, for the one and only time in my life, into an actor. And paid me for it too! If you will agree to call sitting in a chair "acting," it today remains my sole claim to having once been an actor. If you see this fine film on Turner Classic Movies, you can spot me clearly sitting there in my RAF uniform. Everyone else in the scene wore Australian uniforms, for that is where the film was supposed to have been made. (OK, so you won't recognize me. I had hair then.) More importantly, it introduced me to O'Keefe and made him an important part of my later writing career, when he hired me to write his Hollywood TV series, *The Dennis O'Keefe Show.*

Meeting Donald Brian—the Newfoundland star of Broadway who was then in Hollywood making films—gave me the idea for my 2006 book, *Donald Brian, King of Broadway*, which I wrote about his career. It is soon to be made into a major musical in Ontario, set to be released in 2014.

Norma Shearer, a fine actress from Montreal, introduced me to her engineering-genius brother Douglas, who was the first man to bring sound to the big screen.

Because of Fay Wray, I met the king of silent comedy, Mack Sennett, another Canadian, and through him, The Three Stooges. Shemp Howard—who played himself in the trio whenever his brother Curly was too ill to be pushed around, and later took over as an official member of the trio—remained a friend for life. No, they weren't Canadians, but they were great guys. But it was Del Lord from Toronto, director of many of the best *Three Stooges* films, who set me up to receive a pie in the face at the studio when I visited.

I could spend a few pages telling you about the party Mary Pickford gave for me. It was there I met James Cagney, Bette Davis, Eddie Cantor, Olivia de Havilland, Peter Lorre, Ethel Barrymore, Boris Karloff, Groucho Marx, Elizabeth Taylor, Charles Boyer, Basil Rathbone, Mickey Rooney, Judy Garland, Bud Abbott and Lou Costello, Mae West, and Edward G. Robinson. And at my special request, Mary Pickford made sure Shirley Temple and Deanna Durbin were there too. I often wondered if Mary was curious about where I got all the names when she asked me to make a list for her invitations. Actually, I just walked down from Sid Olcott's home to a bookstall on Sunset Boulevard and bought every film magazine I could find, to make sure I missed nobody of importance.

I discovered that Mary was right when she said no one ever refused an invitation to Pickfair. The only three who were on my list but did not come sent telegrams to her apologizing profusely. Thanks to that party, I spent a night at the home of British actor John Loder, and the next morning had my breakfast cooked by his beautiful wife, Hedy Lamarr. I can still describe Hedy in detail, but what I ate for breakfast, I have no idea. The very skimpy negligee she wore while cooking and serving the food made it impossible to even think of eating.

Two more silent-screen giants from London, Ontario—Al and Charles Christie, who once owned the first studio ever built inside Hollywood's city limits—enthralled me for hours with their stories of early movies and the important roles Canadians had played in the birth and growth of Hollywood.

Through Sheila Ryan—never a major headliner, but a contract star at 20th Century Fox and a great friend of the Olcotts—I met Humphrey Bogart and one of the great drummers of the jazz era: Vic Berton from Red Nichols and His Five Pennies. I still have a letter from Vic telling me how he created the name "Five Pennies" for Red Nichols.

When Red created the group, he originally called it a quintet. His agent asked for a more memorable name, and Vic suggested, "since there are five of us and five pennies make a nickel, let's be Red Nichols and His Five Pennies." That name helped make the group unforgettable.

But the days flew by all too quickly, and there soon came a final party at Sid's, to which he and Val invited every Canadian they could find. From 5 P.M. to 3 A.M. I chatted with the elite of Hollywood. On that evening I made friends for life. Jack Warner and Louis B. Mayer, who were both there, told me I had achieved the impossible. "You actually got us an invitation to visit Sid Olcott's home," said Mayer. "This door has been shut to us for years," said Warner.

That night, I lay in bed and wondered if I was simply dreaming that I, a twenty-year-old nobody, had been accepted by the elite of Hollywood as a friend, even a confidante, when I recalled some of the things they had told me. I tapped my head a few times and it was obviously no dream. But I knew it was about to end. Sid and Val planned to drive me to the Los Angeles railroad depot the next morning for the train that would take me directly to Vancouver. They had decided this was better than going through Spokane and on from there to Calgary. They arranged that I would be met in Vancouver by a friend and taken to a hotel overnight before getting the morning train to Calgary.

On my last day, I had Bessie—Sid and Val's cook—drive me to a florist in Hollywood. There, I was finally able to spend some of the money I had brought with me. I sent flowers to more than thirty people with whom I had shared the moments I still recall so vividly. Even though I had still more than enough money in my wallet—my friends hadn't allowed me to spend any during my leave in Hollywood—I found Val and Sid had bought me a first-class train ticket, including a sleeper, for my return trip to Canada. They refused to take a cent from me.

Just as we were about to leave for the station, a car screeched to a stop outside the house. Out jumped Mary Pickford. "I am coming with you to the station," she said. "I wish I could come with you back to Canada. I love it so much. But you have helped bring back so many memories, and I wanted to be here to wish you well."

I quietly shed more than a few tears as the train left the station.

★

From Vancouver, I phoned 37 SFTS in Calgary and told Peter Middleton when I would be arriving back there.

"Gwen and I will meet you," he said. "But we have some news you may not like. Because the next two courses here are both full, you are being transferred to 34 SFTS in Medicine Hat. You will still be flying Harvards, and you should be able to start on a course in Medicine Hat very quickly once you've had a medical and are pronounced fit again."

They were at the station to greet me. "You aren't even going to the base," said Peter. "We are to drive you directly to Medicine Hat. We have had everything packed for you. They are expecting you this afternoon." I was shocked at the decision but obviously I had no choice. Three hours later I was at 34 SFTS. Gwen and Peter stayed to see that everything was fine before they left for the drive back to Calgary.

The officer on duty had been expecting me. He took me to the billet in which I had been allocated a bunk, and told me I was scheduled to meet the station medical officer the next morning at nine. "Once you are pronounced fit again," he said, "We'll see how fast we can get you flying."

Despite the hectic three weeks I had spent in California, I had obviously shaken off the consequences of the rheumatic fever, and at two o'clock the next day the medical officer gave me the good news. "You will be on the next course," he said. "The bad news is that it won't start for two and half weeks. So what are you going to do with yourself?"

It was at this moment that I realized nobody had told him I had just enjoyed the vacation of my life in Hollywood. He was under the impression I had come directly from Harrison Hot Springs and the Colonel Belcher Hospital.

"I understand you had a rough time at the Belcher Hospital, but obviously the time you spent at Harrison Hot Springs has resulted in a complete recovery," he said. "I think maybe you deserve a little vacation. I believe I can get the commanding officer to authorize leave until it is time for the course to start. Have you anywhere you can go for the eighteen days, or do you just want to stay on the base?"

HOW DO YOU TOP HOLLYWOOD?
YOU GO TO NEW YORK

I asked for an hour or two to consider my next move. More leave? It sounded impossible, even though I had enough money in my pocket to enjoy any plan I might dream up.

I suddenly remembered an offer made to me when I was in the Belcher by an American resident physician, Dr. Hal Partington,. He had been as big a swing band enthusiast as I was and often spent the mornings with me listening to Frank Eckersley's radio program. Dr. Partington, not knowing that Peter Middleton would convince me to go to Hollywood, had once offered to contact his good friend, Major Ben Webster at a US Air Corps base in Montana, not far from the Canadian border, if I got leave. He suggested he could arrange for the US Air Force to fly me to New York City so I could perhaps hear some of the big bands live. "They are all playing there," I remembered him saying. So I called him at the Belcher and asked if his offer to contact Major Webster still stood. An hour later I was called to the base office to take a call from the Belcher Hospital. "Ben Webster will arrange everything," he said. "How soon can you be at the US border?"

In less than an hour this amazing doctor had got everything in place. He had contacted Ben Webster and arranged that the major would pick me up at the US border, as long as I could get there from Medicine Hat. This turned out to be very easy. A tip from one of the office staff at 34 SFTS, who heard me talking on the phone, put me in touch with a trucking company in Medicine Hat that sent daily loads across the border into the United States. They agreed instantly to give me a ride if I could be at their office at seven the next morning. I called Dr. Partington back and told him what time I expected to be at the border, and he told me to leave everything else to him and Major Webster. I remember his final words to this day: "Charles, if you get to meet Glenn Miller, tell him that if he had a shrine, I would worship at it!"

My plan worked out so well I had to wait at the border for about thirty minutes for Major Webster to arrive. He was in civilian clothes and driving a Jeep. "I changed so you wouldn't think you had to call me 'sir,'" he said. "RAF shouldn't have to salute anyone. The name is Ben." We shook hands. It didn't seem the time to tell him I had just returned from Hollywood.

On the sixty-minute drive to his Montana air base, he told me what he and Hal Partington had planned. "First," he said, "you will have a quick meal as my guest in the officers' mess. Then at noon you will board a military flight to one of our bases in Ohio. I've made a list of all the people you will meet, complete with telephone numbers in case of emergency. There, they will put you on a transport flight that should get you within twenty miles of New York City around seven this evening. The officer I have listed at the base in New York is a good friend of mine. He will arrange to get you into the city and give you full details on how to contact him for your return flights."

It all sounded so simple. It seemed incredible that my trip could have been arranged so quickly. But it had, and everything went according to plan. Ben Webster was obviously very efficient, and thanks to his contact with Dr. Hal Partington, I had found an amazing new friend. I might well have been Winston Churchill for the VIP treatment I received. At the military airfield near New York they even provided me with a Jeep and a driver to get me into the heart of New York City. Remember, I was still a mere leading aircraftsman—almost the lowest rank in the RAF.

The Jeep driver, Corporal Len Tomlinson, knew New York City well and drove me to a military hostel just off Times Square where he had stayed several times. A comfortable bed cost one dollar a night—and that included breakfast. I checked in around nine o'clock on Sunday night for what I thought would be a fifteen-day stay. But I soon discovered things were not to work out that way.

Len Tomlinson gave me a number to call when I was ready to be picked up again. "Give us forty-eight hours, and we'll have you back in Montana faster than you can say 'Spitfire,'" he said. It is difficult to imagine such things happening today, but there was a generosity and co-operation in the world during the war years that I still look back on with awe and immense satisfaction. How sad it is that this wonderful spirit of goodwill couldn't have continued after the war was over.

I must mention at this point that I gave many US servicemen and -women I met along the way to New York my parents' contact information in Manchester, England, and in the two or three years that followed, my parents played host to more than sixty of the wonderful people I met in 1943, who had been shipped overseas to serve. Happily, Major Ben Webster was one of them. I kept in touch with him for a number of years until, sadly, he died trying to rescue a drowning horse in a lake near Chicago in 1978.

THE CONCERT JIMMY DORSEY PLAYED FOR ME

In 1939 England, when I was only sixteen, the Second World War had already begun and many of the rules about live entertainment on Sundays were relaxed. This gave me the inspiration to hire the best of the British big bands—like Jack Hylton, Henry Hall, Harry Gold, Ambrose, Geraldo, Oscar Rabin, Harry Parry, Joe Loss, and many more—for Sunday concerts in the nearby city of Stockport where my father was, at the time, an alderman.

I booked the bands through an agent, Ed W. Jones, in New Malden, Surrey, and presented them at the 1,600-seat Carlton Theatre. It was just eleven kilometres from Heaton Mersey, where I was then living with my parents following my return home from the circus. In those days, popular bands travelled by bus with all their musicians—often as many as fifteen—plus their singers, and only charged a concert fee amounting to about six hundred Canadian dollars at that time.

I rented the theatre, including its ushers and other staff, for only $100, and for another $10 they even included the theatre organist, Harry D. Speed, who played before the show, during intermission, and while the audience was leaving the theatre. Charging about $1 for the tickets I made $1,600 from each show. If, as was always the case, the evening show sold out quickly, I added an afternoon performance—that, too, never had an empty seat. The band charged an extra $200 for the second show, and the theatre another $40. Under the government's new Sunday concert rules, 75 percent of all box-office receipts had to go to a charity. I chose the British Limbless Ex-Servicemen's Association (BLESMA), since wounded soldiers, sailors, and airmen were already starting to come home from the war.

At each concert I paid ten dollars to a young Manchester BBC Radio news announcer to emcee the shows. He didn't own a car, and arrived for each concert on the bus. He appeared at every one of my shows, but never had his name on the posters. He later went on to considerable fame as an actor on stage and radio, and in films and television. His name was Wilfred Pickles! (By the way, the ten dollars covered appearances at both shows, but I did always invite him to my parents' home for supper in between.)

I must tell you that Wilfred Pickles, in his later years of fame, did something few other people have been generous enough to do. His father had become bankrupt many years earlier, when an associate defrauded him of a great deal of money. Wilfred took it on himself to find out the names and addresses of all those who lost money in the company's collapse and paid off every penny of his father's debt, with interest. He was a great man whom I recall well to this day.

In two years—not taking a cent for myself after deducting the band costs and theatre rental—I was able to hand around 85 percent of the box-office over to BLESMA. My gift totaled more than $72,000, a huge sum in those days.

I remember the horrified look on Jack Hylton's face when he arrived at the theatre to discover he had signed a contract with a sixteen-year-old. But I gave him his fee in cash, as I did with all the bandleaders; and after he had spoken on the phone to agent Ed Jones, who told him there had never been the slightest problem with me, we became friends. Such good friends that when Hylton's orchestra was scheduled to appear at a series of dances in the Manchester area he insisted that Ed Jones allow me to negotiate all the individual contracts with the dance halls. I was paid 10 percent of each deal.

Sitting in the saxophone section of the Jack Hylton Orchestra that night was a young man who pretended to play: he couldn't read a note of music. Throughout the concert, he did a lot of crazy things—like knocking over music stands or tripping over a microphone and falling flat on the stage—that added a touch of superb comedy to the entire evening. Jack Hylton was the only big band leader who had such a comic in the band and it was a great success. I remember telling the comedian during the intermission that I loved his sense of humour and thought he had all the potential to become very famous in his own right in the future.

Two years later, we met again when the young man was appearing as a solo stand-up comic at the Theatre Royal in Stockport. He spent quite a bit of time at my home each day. He had not become famous yet, but it certainly did happen eventually. Ernie Wise teamed up with Eric Morecambe and as "Morecambe and Wise." They became big stars in England and appeared many times on *The Ed Sullivan Show* in New York.

We were still friends in the 1960s when the two fine comics appeared at the O'Keefe Centre in Toronto as stars of the London Palladium Show. I took Ernie and Eric out to dinner after one of the performances. "You were the first person who ever told me I might be successful," said Ernie. "I shall never forget those concerts in Stockport."

★

Thoroughly enchanted with the sounds of the British big bands of that era, I was excited when the RAF sent me to Canada to learn to fly. I wasn't sure how far New York was from Canada, but I hoped I would get there to see and hear some of the great American bands like Glenn Miller, the Dorsey Brothers, Benny Goodman, and Guy Lombardo.

I had been reading *Downbeat,* the number-one music industry magazine, from the day I arrived in Canada and now, when this opportunity to visit New York arrived, I knew exactly where every band would be playing in the big city or nearby. I had discovered from *Downbeat* that the Jimmy Dorsey Orchestra was playing at Frank Dailey's famed Meadowbrook Ballroom at Cedar Grove in nearby New Jersey. A friendly volunteer at the service hostel helped me get there by listing all the right subway trains to get me to the doors of the ballroom.

It was about five in the evening when I arrived outside the entrance.

It was early and everything was still shuttered. Posters advertising *The Jimmy Dorsey Orchestra* were clearly displayed, so I decided to wait until the doors opened. Looking at photographs of the band and singers Helen O'Connell and Bob Eberly, I suddenly spotted an extra poster that was almost a heart-stopper.

These were the words that stunned me: *MEADOWBROOK BALL-ROOM CLOSED EVERY MONDAY UNTIL FURTHER NOTICE.*

It was Monday.

A dream was shattered. I was ready to head back to New York very saddened when the double doors suddenly opened behind me and I was knocked to the ground by a rush of people exiting the ballroom. The man who picked me up was unmistakably the great bandleader Jimmy Dorsey. "Hey fella," he said. "Sorry, but we've had a long rehearsal and just wanted to smell fresh air and go home." He looked at my uniform. "Is that a Royal Air Force uniform you are wearing? Are you in the Royal Air Force?"

By now all the musicians had gathered around. None had boarded the band bus that had drawn in beside the curb.

"Yes," I responded. "I'm in the RAF."

"First I've ever met," said Dorsey. "What are you doing here?"

"Well, I was hoping to hear you guys play," I said. "It's my first day on leave in New York and I've never heard an American band except on records. But I see the ballroom is closed tonight. Hopefully I'll be able to come back another night."

Jimmy Dorsey looked slyly at his musicians and singers. Then he smiled and raised his hands. "Fellas," he said, "I think we need at least one more hour's rehearsal. There were some rather ragged spots today." Without a word of protest the musicians carried their instruments back into the ballroom and in minutes were set up onstage. "Change into band uniforms," said Dorsey. "This has to be the real thing."

Like lambs, those star musicians went to the dressing rooms and in minutes were back onstage. "Have we got sound and lighting?" yelled Dorsey.

Voices answered, "Yes, Mr. Dorsey."

Dorsey dragged a chair off the stage and placed it right in the middle of the beautiful ballroom. "Sit there and relax," he said. "You're going to have your own special one-hour concert of the Jimmy Dorsey Orchestra all to yourself. You took the trouble to come and see us, so see and hear us you will."

I wasn't exactly alone. About a dozen cleaners and other ballroom employees sat on the floor around me for the greatest concert of my life. When Helen O'Connell and Bob Eberly sang "Green Eyes," Helen called me onstage and sang that last chorus about two inches from my face. Then she kissed me and said, "You really do have green eyes!"

"Wanna do that number again?" asked Dorsey.

"Yes please," I said.

Helen hugged me while Bob Eberly sang his part; then she came so very close for the final chorus that it gave me a few minutes of near-paradise.

The show went on for sixty minutes. They played all the Dorsey hits including "Six Lessons from Madame La Zonga," "The Breeze and I," "I Understand," "Amapola," and of course, "Tangerine." Then I stood up, exhausted from applauding, cheering, and the nearness of Helen O'Connell, and told Jimmy Dorsey it was a day I would never forget, but that I couldn't let the tired musicians weary themselves any more. That was when the band stood up and applauded *me*.

"We're going back to New York on our bus," said Jimmy. "Wanna ride with us?"

Did I? During the trip I collected all their autographs on a piece of paper the driver provided. They dropped me right at the door of my service hostel. Everyone got off the bus to shake hands with me before waving from open windows as the bus drove away. The bus said *The Jimmy Dorsey Orchestra* in large letters, and a big crowd gathered, obviously wondering who on earth I was being given such treatment.

I was relaxing in my room a half-hour later when a knock on the door told me I was wanted at the reception desk to take a phone call. I was startled. Who could possibly know I was there? I had no idea.

"Hi RAF guy," said an unknown voice. "My name is Russ Case. I'm a musician. Jimmy Dorsey called me a few minutes ago and asked me to take charge of you while you are in New York. You want to see the big bands? I'll pick you up at eight in the morning for breakfast and we'll get started."

I had no idea who Russ Case was, but remembering my remarkable experience in Hollywood with the Olcotts, I said, "Yes please," without any hesitation. And that was the start of a second incredible vacation, when I had the chance to meet many important people in the world of music and hear some great performers live onstage. To this day, I can still recall with delight my first astonishing visit to the great city of New York.

ΡUSS CASE OPENED ONE HUNDRED
MUSICAL DOORS IN NEW YORK

When we first became friends in 1943, Russell "Russ" Case, the former Benny Goodman Orchestra star trumpet player, was leading his own radio orchestra called the Million Dollar Band five nights a week on NBC Radio in New York. I was waiting outside the service centre the next morning when a bright red convertible screeched to a stop at the front door. The driver spotted my uniform and shouted at me to get in the car. "I'm Russ," he said. "Welcome to our city."

That morning, and almost every other morning at eight, I met Russ and a group of New York's finest musicians in the coffee shop attached to the NBC Radio City Studios. All of them were from the big bands or studio bands working in New York. Many of the musicians were in uniform. Glenn Miller had already volunteered to join the United States Army Air Corps (USAAC), and more than a dozen of the great musicians who had made his orchestra number one had gone along with him.

The Miller Orchestra performed their daily radio shows from the CBS Radio Studios (just off Times Square at 53rd Street in New York City), live in the US and Canada and broadcast overseas to American forces in about two dozen different countries. Most of the band earned additional pay by working in the studios as members of the groups that accompanied singers like Dick Haymes, Helen O'Connell, and the wonderful Andrews Sisters, who did live shows every day of the week. Often their uniforms could be seen onstage in Russ Case's Million Dollar Band.

I recall the first morning I was asked to join them. Russ Case turned to me and said, "Hey, Charles, do you object to coloured people?"

"Object?" I said. "Of course not, they are no different to anyone else. Why do you ask?"

"Wasn't sure what you RAFers felt about coloureds," said Russ. "There are a lot playing great music here and I have one I especially want you to meet." Russ beckoned over a man sitting a few seats away from me. "The greatest jazz drummer in the world," he said. "Cozy, this is my RAF pal, Charlie Foster. Charlie, this is Cozy Cole. Nobody keeps a steadier beat than this guy." We shook hands, and started a friendship that lasted until Cozy died forty years later at his beautiful home in northern New York State, which I was privileged to visit many times.

★

After the war, when I was working as publicity director for Jack Kent Cooke at CKEY Radio in Toronto, a 45 rpm disc was dropped on my desk by Mr. Cooke. "I understand you know this man," he said. The disk, labeled *Topsy*, was by Cozy Cole and his quintet of top jazz musicians. "Doesn't fit our Top 40 programming," he continued, "but I thought you might like it."

I put it on the turntable in my office and we both listened to Cozy's great beat. I heard what I believed was a superb record. "Jack," I said, "maybe it doesn't fit, but it should. CKEY could make this into a big hit."

Jack looked very doubtful, but agreed to do me a favour. "I'll have Don Insley put it on everyone's playlist," he said. "We'll give it three days, but if our audiences don't like it, that's the end of it."

Within hours our phones were ringing, asking for more plays of Cozy's new record. Within a week, every other station in Toronto was playing it. The record flew off the music store shelves and *Downbeat* printed the story—I made sure of that. New York disc jockey Alan Freed read the story and suddenly, thanks to his acceptance and promotion, Cozy's record became number one across both Canada and the United States. *Topsy*, and later *Topsy 2*, put Cozy Cole back in the spotlight. He had done little after the war when the big bands dissolved, and suddenly he and his group were back to headlining in clubs and theatres.

It was as satisfying to me as it was to him. To have repaid his wartime friendship in this way is one of my life's most rewarding memories. When he came to Toronto to thank CKEY for making his record a hit, it was my turn to make sure he had the time of his life.

★

This story really isn't about Russ or Cozy, but Cozy was unintentionally involved in me missing out on getting an autograph that probably would be quite a collector's item today. We were chatting in the NBC restaurant when Cozy asked if there were any musicians there I hadn't seen and met before. He knew my autograph book was overflowing with signatures, as he and Russ made sure I talked with everyone.

"Don't think I've been introduced to that man over there at the end of the counter," I said.

"He's not a musician," said Cozy when I pointed to the rather plump man downing, at eight in the morning, a large glass of whisky. (From the look of the counter in front of him, it wasn't by any means his first.) "He likes to drink and he likes musicians so we let him join us when he's in town. He often has some great stories to tell, so we enjoy having him here. But he isn't a musician, so we didn't think you would be interested."

A few days later, when I hadn't seen the unknown for a while, I casually asked Russ Case what had happened to him.

"Don't think we'll see him for a while," he said, "He is out on a westcoast swing to promote something or other."

"What does he do?" I asked.

"He used to play baseball. He was one of the big ones, but he's retired now," said Russ. "You don't play baseball in England, do you?" he said. "Cricket's your game, isn't it? I doubt you've ever heard of Babe Ruth."

I hadn't. And that, sadly, is why I never did get the baseball legend's autograph.

MY CARNEGIE HALL
BIG BAND "DEBUT"

Every day in New York, I was given the royal treatment by the most renowned musicians in the city. Glenn Miller, already in the US Army Air Corps, was based there. Russ Morgan, Jimmy Dorsey, Guy Lombardo, Bob Chester, Jimmy Lunceford, and Benny Goodman were playing at the most prestigious theatres and hotels in the city and making daily broadcasts to servicemen and -women overseas. I visited radio studios, theatres, nightclubs, and restaurants to hear music and meet musicians of world renown. But it was my greatest thrill when I was invited to a radio broadcast at Carnegie Hall.

For more than one hundred years, musicians of the world—from the classical giants to the jazz geniuses, and even the rock and rollers who can't read music—have all hoped one day they would appear on-stage at one of the most prestigious music venues of all time: Carnegie Hall. It was Benny Goodman and his big band that broke the rule that only classical music was to be played in the beautiful and acoustically perfect hall. Today, anyone with enough money to pay the substantial rental costs can make an appearance. (One insignificant rock group did just that in 2011, and played to a totally empty house. They forget to advertise the concert.)

Russ Case made my visit to Carnegie Hall possible, but it turned out to be much more than a simple visit. Although he had his own Million Dollar Band and a popular radio program, he still found time to play with other orchestras. First-class trumpet players were in short supply during the war years and Russ was one of the best. He was not the only bandleader to drop his baton and play as a mere member of the band whenever he was needed. I recall, at one broadcast of the Million Dollar Band, seeing two of the greatest clarinetists of all time, Benny Goodman and Artie Shaw, sitting onstage and playing in the band as if they were just two ordinary musicians. So I was not surprised at the end of my first week when Russ invited me to Carnegie Hall, where he was to play in the André Kostelanetz Orchestra for its regular Coca Cola radio show, *The Pause That Refreshes.*

I looked around as the orchestra set up onstage and recognized friends like trumpeter Billy Butterfield, drummer Cozy Cole, trombonist Lou McGarrity, and several musicians from the Glenn Miller Air Corps band, including bassist Trigger Alpert. Like Russ and his NBC band, Kostelanetz depended on musicians from other orchestras during the war, when most of his own musicians had been called up for military service. I expected to sit in the audience to watch the rehearsals and performance, but was delighted when Russ came down to me and said, "We've put another chair in the brass section. You can sit with us for the rehearsal and concert. You read music, so we've put you up a music stand. You'll unofficially be third trumpet, though of course you won't play!"

A studio conductor took the rehearsal and even though I wasn't playing I was able to exchange sly grins with my friends as I heard them play occasional wrong notes on first runs-through of the music. When Kostelanetz arrived, just before three o'clock, he looked over the sixty musicians, nodding approvingly at the high standard of players present. He talked with many of them before spotting me sitting in my RAF uniform between Billy and Russ. The rehearsal conductor whispered to him how I came to be there. He looked rather severe as he walked across the front of the stage and climbed up to where I was seated. Russ gave me a pat on the back and whispered loudly, "He can't eat you, pal!"

Kostelanetz broke into a smile, put out his hand, and grabbed mine in a firm handshake. "The British Royal Air Force," he said, "is a dignified and noble organization. I welcome you to my orchestra. I am proud to have you here."

Russ chimed in: "André," he said, "he reads music. I thought he would appreciate the experience."

"I have no objection," said Kostelanetz. He asked me a few questions about my flying school in Alberta. "Can you receive our program in your camp at Medicine Hat?" he asked.

I told him that RAF pilot trainees at every station across Canada never missed his weekly show, and that in Bowden it was always aired in the station dining hall.

"Then I shall try to make this day a memorable one for you," he said.

At that moment, I had no idea how memorable.

What a difference when Kostelanetz took over the baton. The orchestra suddenly sounded more exciting, more decisive. There were no wrong notes—at least not in the brass section, because I followed the music very carefully.

Sitting in with the orchestra was a great experience, but it was the closing words of the show from Andre Kostelanetz that made it a memory I shall never forget.

"Thank you for being with us today," he told his millions of listeners from coast to coast in North America. "I would be remiss if I did not tell you that we had the privilege of having a special guest sitting in our trumpet section today. Charles Foster, a young member of the British Royal Air Force, now stationed at 34 Service Flying Training School in Medicine Hat, Alberta, in beautiful Canada, has joined us for this one occasion. Soon he will return to his flying training, but we look forward to welcoming him back once this terrible war is over."

When the red light went off signalling that we were off the air, I went up to André Kostelanetz. "It was remarkable," I said, "the difference when you took over the baton. It reminded me of the contrast in the playing of the London Philharmonic Orchestra when Sir Thomas Beecham takes over from the rehearsal conductor." I recall adding that I had experienced many such rehearsals, since Sir Thomas was my Uncle Tommy.

His eyes lit up. "I can't ever before remember having had such a significant tribute paid to me," he said. He held up his hands for silence and repeated to the entire orchestra and audience, still sitting in their seats, what I had said. "I regard Sir Thomas as the greatest conductor in the world," he said.

ESSEX HOUSE HOTEL,
HERE I COME

I was really very comfortable in the service hostel that I had found on my arrival in New York and had enjoyed the treatment I had received there during my first week, so I was a little astonished when Russ Case and big bandleader Russ Morgan arrived at the end of my first week with instructions to pack my belongings: they were taking me somewhere else to stay for the rest of my leave.

I think I protested a little. The staff at the hostel had been superb. The free breakfasts were a bonus, and at one dollar a night I couldn't imagine anything that could possibly be better.

Until I reached my new accommodations provided by the two Russes.

Russ Morgan's car, into which I had piled my belongings, took me to one of the city's most luxurious hotels: Essex House, overlooking the wonderful Central Park.

"I can't afford to stay here," I protested.

"You don't have to 'afford' anything," said Russ Morgan. "This is where I live while I'm in New York. I have a second bedroom I keep for friends and guests. That room is yours for the rest of your stay and there will be no hotel charges. All your meals will be free. The management has agreed that a member of the British Royal Air Force deserves no less."

The room I found myself in was lavish. It wasn't simply a "room," it was a suite with a sitting room, bedroom, and everything else that goes with sheer luxury. The service at Essex House was incredible. The staff—and I discovered by talking to them that at least half were Canadian—fell over themselves to make sure I had everything I wanted. I was delighted to discover that living in the next suite was the great British singer and entertainer Gracie Fields. Russ just knocked on her door and the friendly Gracie invited us in for a chat. "I'm from Lancashire too," said Gracie. "Whatever you want, just ask me, I'll see you get it immediately." Happily, thanks to so many other remarkable show business personalities in New York, I never had to ask her for anything. But I did enjoy dinner with her one evening before she took me to the Roxy Theatre, where she was appearing nightly to packed audiences.

When the hotel manager knocked on my door and simply said he wanted to make sure everything was perfect, I knew I had landed in heaven.

I HAD TO ASK WHO
FRANK SINATRA WAS IN 1943

It seems impossible even now, seven decades after he reached his greatest fame, to imagine anyone would dare ask: "Who is this Frank Sinatra?" But I made that terrible blunder when Russ Case was playing trumpet in the Lucky Strike *Your Hit Parade* radio show orchestra: I thought I should go along with him to the morning rehearsal because it might be possible to meet Frank Sinatra.

"He's a good friend of mine," said Russ. "With a bit of luck, he'll have time after the rehearsal to have lunch with us."

"Who is this Frank Sinatra everyone talks about?" I asked. "I gather he is quite important and I think I may have heard some of his records, but I really don't know anything about him."

I don't think I have ever seen anyone's jaw drop as low as did Russ's at that moment.

"You don't know who Frank Sinatra is?" he gasped.

"Well, I know he is a singer who was with bands like Harry James," I said. "But I really don't know much about him. Is he still singing with one of the big bands?"

"Oh, dear no!" said Russ. "Frankie will never be singing with a big band again. Wait till you hear the audience at *Your Hit Parade*. When he walks onstage, you'll see why. Every young girl in the United States swoons when he sings. Frank Sinatra is today the greatest singer of popular music in the world."

I was ashamed to tell him that war-torn England hadn't yet realized this young singer was so important.

When we arrived at the stage door, we had to fight our way through the crowds of young girls who were waiting there to see Sinatra.

He hadn't arrived when the orchestra set up onstage for rehearsals. But after twenty minutes there was no doubt he was in the theatre. The screams from outside echoed through CBS Radio Studio No. 3 at 1697 Broadway. They were so loud that when the stage door opened the musicians stopped playing and the rehearsal came to a stop. Sitting in the audience, I suddenly saw a group of uniformed guards holding onto a tousled-haired young man who looked as though he had been rescued from near death.

Frank Sinatra had arrived!

The screams subsided as the stage door was closed. Sinatra thanked the guards who had brought him in and headed for his dressing room. Obviously this was an everyday happening at a *Your Hit Parade* rehearsal. The music restarted and I sat back to listen. Suddenly I realized I was not alone. Putting his hand out to greet me was the young man who had so noisily arrived ten minutes earlier.

"Hi," he said. "I'm Frank Sinatra. Russ said you were here as his guest, and since I've never met anyone in the British Royal Air Force before I thought I should come over and see you before they need me for rehearsal."

It was an hour before they needed him, and within that time I came to the conclusion that while this amazing young singer was one of the biggest radio and recording stars in the United States, he was also a very down-to-earth gentleman and a remarkably nice guy. Russ and I joined Frank for lunch in his dressing room. It was very informal: hot dogs. Outside the room were two uniformed guards.

As the afternoon rehearsal progressed I began to understand why "Frankie" was so adored in the United States. Not only was his voice superb, but his entire attitude toward everyone was so understanding and co-operative that, though he was a star, to everyone in the theatre—from the cleaners to the great musicians who made *Your Hit*

Parade so memorable—he was just a wonderful guy who seemed to have a magic that no one else had.

After the rehearsal, he walked offstage down to me in the audience.

"You've been very patient sitting here," he said. "What say you and I have a bit of fun before the big show tonight? I want you to go out the stage door, find a couple of the prettiest young ladies you can find, bring them in—I'll arrange that you can do this without trouble—and we'll all slip out a side entrance and have supper at my hotel, the Waldorf Astoria."

"*Us?*" I asked. "Why on earth us? There must be hundreds of people you could take out to eat."

"You are my first RAF man. I like you. I need a friend who will answer me truthfully, just as you did a few hours ago when I asked you if you thought I was the best singer in the United States, and you said, 'I'll tell you when I have heard you, but right now I am a Bing Crosby fan.' Nobody in two years has dared tell me that. I think we will be good friends if you promise to always tell me the truth."

I promised. And I kept that promise throughout the many years of our friendship that followed.

I went out the stage door into the mob of hundreds of young ladies standing there screaming. It wasn't easy but I chose two of the quietest and told them I could take them to Sinatra if they followed me. It was their answer that convinced me that I had selected two of the best.

"Oh yes," said Sue Bonner, "and what do we have to do for you? Judy and I aren't that type of girl, forget it."

I promised there would be no demands, and maybe the RAF uniform convinced them to follow me. The security man at the stage door had been alerted and he opened the door to let us in.

After Sue Bonner and Judy West had recovered from the shock of actually meeting Sinatra, we headed out of the theatre quietly through a side door into a waiting car and the four of us enjoyed a great meal in a quiet room at the Waldorf Astoria Hotel where Frank was staying and also appearing nightly in the hotel's Wedgwood Room.

When we got back to the radio theatre, the girls were given front-row seats with me, and after the broadcast we were escorted back to

Sinatra's dressing room. He stayed and talked with us for nearly an hour at the end of a ten-hour day. I know Sue and Judy never forgot that day, because I kept in touch with them by mail for more than ten years, until, tragically, both drowned in a swimming pool disaster while on vacation with their husbands in the Bahamas.

I knew for certain that Frank Sinatra was no ordinary man at seven the next morning, when the phone rang in my suite at Essex House.

"Hi, my friend," said the now unmistakable voice of Sinatra. "I'll be up there in about an hour. I'm bringing my tailor, Lew Epstein, with me. I was worried about your uniform yesterday. It needs work. Can't have you running around New York looking like that. Have you something to change into while Lew works on the one you were wearing?"

I said I had a second jacket and trousers. "Great," said Sinatra. "Then he can take away that awful one from yesterday and work on it. Don't worry, he is brilliant; and though they may look at the uniform back at your camp and wonder why it looks so good, they will never know what has happened to it. Rely on it: Lew is the greatest. He will work on it all day, and tomorrow will take away your other uniform and fix that too." Despite being astonished and concerned as to what my RAF uniforms might look like at the end of Lew Epstein's work, I didn't even think of arguing.

Lew and Frank arrived at Essex House fifty minutes later, just as I was finishing breakfast in my room. Frank just sat and talked about many things, and told me about his personal life and his hope to one day visit England, while Lew measured me from top to bottom and smiled as he promised "a uniform tomorrow that will be so good, you'll look like a general." I had other things to do that day, and Frank obviously did too. By nine o'clock I was on my way in my second outfit ready to enjoy another day organized by Russ Case.

When I arrived back at Essex House at eleven that night, a package was waiting for me at the front desk. I opened it, and could hardly believe my eyes. My RAF uniform—the same one so badly creased and rumpled the day before—had been transformed. Frank Sinatra was right: Lew Epstein was a master tailor.

There was a note attached telling me to leave my second uniform at the desk to be collected the next morning. So when I was ready to leave the next day on a rather unexpected trip to Washington, DC, I was wearing the best-looking RAF uniform ever made. As it turned out, in view of who I met, this was most appropriate.

THANKS TO COZY COLE, I MET TWO REMARKABLE PEOPLE IN WASHINGTON

Although it was Russ Case, who later in his great career became musical director for singer Perry Como, who did the most to make my leave in New York unforgettable, it was Cozy Cole who helped create one unexpected memory that is still fresh in my mind today.

Cozy Cole was the first black man I had ever met. Although I did meet many more from the musical world during my two weeks in New York, it was Cozy whose attitude towards life I quickly came to admire. We remained in touch for almost four decades until, sadly, he died on January 31, 1981.

Segregation was very strong in New York City in the 1940s. Despite his fame, Cozy often had to walk home after playing late at night, because white taxi drivers would not pick him up. At that time in his illustrious career, Cozy was playing onstage only in the great black bands led by the likes of Lionel Hampton and Cab Calloway; but behind the scenes of the music industry musicians and singers who were more concerned with talent than colour, and he and other fine black entertainers were accepted everywhere by everyone.

I remember Cozy walking back to Essex House with me after an afternoon radio show, only to find I could not invite him in to dine with me because "coloured men" were not allowed in the hotel. I was so annoyed I yelled for the manager and got mad for the one and only time during my stay in that great city. When I told the manager I would pack my bags if Cozy was not allowed into the dining room, I was astonished to hear applause coming from all the people who were standing around.

As a result, Cozy Cole was the first black man ever to dine at Essex House. The staff seemed delighted, and the manager later told me he planned to urge the hotel owners to open their doors to everyone from that day on. But I believe it was quite a time before that happened.

When I met Cozy in Toronto after the war, he told me it was one of the most enjoyable moments of his life. "I never thought it could happen," he told me. "You changed the world that day." So in 1943, when Cozy suggested that I fly with him and his quartet of black musicians to Washington, where he was to play at a charity concert to raise money to provide scholarships for black university students, I said, "Yes please!"

Cozy's black quartet was to be augmented by a number of top black Washington musicians. They would accompany the other artists (all black) who were appearing, and they planned to spend a few hours rehearsing with the performers. I should mention that I believe I was the only white person in the theatre that day. Even the ushers and stage crew were black. For some reason, probably because Cozy had brought me there, I was accepted.

★

The flight was uneventful, and once in the theatre in Washington, Cozy suggested I might like to see a little of the city. "Why not take a walk along Pennsylvania Avenue to the White House?" he said. "Who knows, you might see the president's dog, Fala, running around the grounds."

Ten minutes later, I was standing outside the iron fence that surrounded the White House, wondering if President Roosevelt was actually inside, when a soft voice interrupted my daydream. "Are you stationed in Washington with the Royal Air Force?" asked the unknown lady.

I swung around to see a smiling middle-aged lady, wearing what seemed like one of the old-fashioned hats my mother wore back in England on Sundays to go to church. I smiled back. "No, I'm just here for one day and thought I might look to see if the president's dog might be running around outside."

"Is that all you want to see?" asked my new acquaintance.

"Of course it would be wonderful to see the president himself, but I'm sure he will be much too busy to see me."

"Well, why don't we see if he is too busy?" said the smiling lady. She grasped me by the arm and, rather hesitantly, I walked with her along the White House fence to where it ended and a roadway turned in toward what was obviously an entrance to the building.

When we reached what appeared to be a guardhouse I expected the security men would bar our way and that would be the end of my dream. But they didn't. They actually saluted us and we passed through the checkpoint as though it were the easiest thing in the world to get in to see the president of the United States.

"How did you do that?" I asked my companion.

"You'd be surprised what a smile can do," she replied.

We walked along a lengthy corridor before we reached a reception room with two curved staircases leading up to what looked like a small balcony. Beyond it I could see a door.

My unknown companion headed to the stairs. "Sit down and relax," she said. "I'll just go and see if the president can spare a few moments to talk with you."

Before I could ask who she was to be able to work such miracles, she was bounding up the stairs, and someone I couldn't see opened the door for her. Minutes later, the door opened again and a huge black man dressed in a magnificent uniform came out on the balcony. "Please come up," he said, "The president will see you now."

By now I was in a complete daze. Once through the door I followed my uniformed companion along a corridor to a door at which he knocked. A voice called out: "Enter."

I entered to see, sitting in front of me behind a huge desk, Franklin Delano Roosevelt, the president of the United States. Without getting up, he put out his hand for me to shake. He then waved me into a huge chair near the desk. I wondered why he had not stood up, but thought perhaps presidents didn't stand for mere mortals such as me. Word had not reached us in England about the polio that had plagued him for much of his life.

He asked why I was in Washington and I explained to him that Cozy Cole had invited me as his guest. "Wonderful musician," said the president. "I saw him playing in New York with Cab Calloway's Orchestra, but have never had the good fortune to meet him."

He picked up the phone. "Get me a photographer," said the president. "I need him here in five minutes."

He asked about my training as a pilot. He wanted to know about my family. He asked my mother's name, and jotted it down with the address he also requested. It was months later before I knew he had handwritten a personal letter to my mother to say he had met me.

The photographer arrived. "Come and stand by me, Charles," said President Roosevelt. It was at this moment that I realized he was in a wheelchair, but I didn't dare ask why.

A few minutes later, my visit with the president was over. We shook hands again. The uniformed attendant showed me out as three rather important men carrying briefcases entered the room. He escorted me down the stairs and pointed my way along the corridor to the exit through which I had entered.

I thanked him for his courtesy. "Don't thank me," he said, "it is Mrs. Eleanor Roosevelt you should thank."

"Mrs. Roosevelt?" I questioned aloud. "What did she have to do with it?"

"It was she who brought you in," he said. "That's her way. She walks among the ordinary people and never seeks glory. But without her, our president would not be a whole man."

★

Back at the theatre, I awaited a break in rehearsals before going backstage.

"Cozy, you are not going to believe me," I started to say.

He held up his hand to interrupt. "I know," he said, "You've been talking to President Roosevelt."

"How on earth did you know that? I asked.

"The president called me a few moments before you got back," he said. "He wished me luck with the concert and said he would have liked to be here, but the pressure of work is too great. But he is sending over a cheque for our cause."

Later that evening I saw the cheque. The president was very generous.

I have often wondered if President Roosevelt noticed how smartly I was dressed in my new Lew Epstein uniform. Hopefully he did, and thought my smart appearance was normal in the RAF.

★

When I returned home to England, I saw the busy President Roosevelt had found time to use the English address of my parents that he had asked for. On the dining room fireplace mantle was a beautifully framed, handwritten letter from the president, in which he said I was looking well and enjoying North America. With it was the photograph taken of the two of us in his office on that memorable day in Washington. (I must confess being very proud of how smart I looked in my Lew Epstein RAF uniform.)

My parents would never part with the picture or the letter, and although I have tried my hardest to find them over the years, I have never been able to discover where they went when my father finally left this earth.

GLENN MILLER'S BAND
KEPT A PROMISE

It is difficult to select highlights from my wartime RAF leave in New York City without leaving out people who deserve mention for giving me the time of my life. And there were so many. Long before I reached England with my wings as a Royal Air Force pilot, members of the wonderful Glen Miller Orchestra had given my parents, back home in England, a day they talked about all their lives. Russ Case was the catalyst for everything that happened, but his sit-in role in the Glenn Miller Orchestra trumpet section, which had been depleted by illness, opened a special door that didn't close when I left New York.

Glenn Miller had joined the United States Army Air Corps about a month before I arrived in New York. Most of his civilian musicians were with him, but a few new members were added, including a string section that became, for the first time, part of the orchestra. Hollywood actor Broderick Crawford, then in the US forces, became the announcer for the band's radio shows, which were recorded daily and syndicated around the world wherever American or Allied soldiers could hear them.

Singer Tony Martin—already an established film personality who had volunteered to join the US Army Air Corps—was guest singer, although Johnny Desmond was the main band singer. The band members were busy having inoculations and medical checks in New York when I first met them. Two of the Miller trumpet players had bad reactions to the shots, and Glenn Miller asked Russ Case and Billy Butterfield—two of the best civilian trumpeters in the city—to sit in for a few days while they recovered. Russ took me along to rehearsals and introduced me to Miller and many of the Miller musicians he had worked with in peacetime.

Glenn Miller told me he chose Russ and Billy because he knew they would need little rehearsal before fitting in perfectly with the "Miller sound." Incredibly, they did. Seeing brand new music charts for the first time, they didn't blow a false note at first run-through. "Brilliant," said Miller. "We didn't even need to rehearse that one!"

Jimmy Priddy, Miller's lead trombone in both his civilian and military bands, became my special friend. He and I found we not only loved New York and the Miller music, but animals too. What little time he had to spare we spent at the Bronx Zoo, admiring and feeding the animals so wonderfully cared for there.

I saw a lot of Broderick Crawford and Tony Martin since they were not onstage all the time. Tony drove me around the city in his sleek convertible, pointing out places he knew and little clubs in which he had worked before Hollywood fame found him.

Brod Crawford was a food expert. He knew every decent restaurant in the city and I enjoyed many meals with him.

Trigger Alpert, the excitable bass player with an incredible sense of humour, and Ray McKinley, the brilliant drummer who later led both his own band and the Miller band after the war, became special pals of mine.

Before I left New York, Jimmy Priddy asked for my parents' address in England. "We'll be over there before you," he said. "I'll call them to say you are doing fine over here." That promise became much more than a mere telephone call. When I returned home to England with my coveted RAF pilot's wings, my mother told me the following story.

★

MRS. FOSTER, WE WONDER IF WE MIGHT PAY YOU A VISIT?
(AS TOLD BY CHARLES FOSTER'S MOTHER)

The phone rang one day and a Mr. Jimmy Priddy, who said he was with the Glenn Miller Orchestra in London, called to say he had seen you in New York and that you would soon be home. He said that he and the band had been shocked to find food so short in England, and wondered if it would be acceptable if he and a few members of the orchestra drove up to our home at the weekend to bring us a few supplies, which they seemed to have on their base in plenty.

Now, we all knew the great Glenn Miller band was in England, but I had no idea you had become friendly with them in New York or that your father and I, who loved their music, would ever meet them. So I said they would be very welcome. Two days later, five Jeeps arrived at our house at 42 Queen's Drive in Heaton Mersey and out jumped more than a dozen members of the band.

Mr. Miller wasn't with them, but after Mr. Priddy told us of your adventures in America, he asked if they might play a short concert on our front lawn. By then all the neighbours had come out to see why the Jeeps were there. Once people discovered it was the Glenn Miller band, we quickly had several hundred people crowding round.

They got out their instruments, and we pushed our grand piano to the front of the living room and opened all the windows. Mr. Mel Powell played piano inside the house and the rest of the twelve musicians sat on the sloping lawn outside. Their music drew an even bigger crowd and the concert lasted more than an hour before Mr. Priddy told us they must return to London.

They signed hundreds of autographs, and I specially recall Mr. Vince Carbone, a saxophone player, because he gave everyone his New York telephone number and asked anyone who might go over the Atlantic after the war to call him—a meal would be ready on his table for anyone who visited. Mr. Broderick Crawford, the actor, who was with them, sat with your father and me listening to the music. Everyone crowded round for his autograph.

Then they ended the concert with what will long be remembered in Heaton Mersey as an astonishing gesture. Out of all the Jeeps, they pulled box after box of food of every kind. When we finally got them unpacked, we couldn't believe our eyes. There were more chocolate bars in one box than we had seen in three years. Your father took those over the next day to the children's ward of the Stockport hospital and he said he was sure the sight alone helped get a lot of youngsters healthy again. There was too much food for just us with you and Pat (my mother's sister) away at war, so we shared it with neighbours and gave a big party for the old people in a seniors' home in Stockport.

Next day I received a telephone call from Mr. Miller. He said how much he regretted not being present, but that a military commitment had made it impossible. He said you had become a good friend in New York and that as soon as we heard you were back in England again we must tell you that you should call him immediately at a number I have in Bedford, where the band is staying over here.

It was a great day in our lives. Newspapers were on our doorstep for days, asking lots of questions. Why were we chosen? When we told them you had met the band in New York, you became quite famous; but of course nobody was able to get in touch with you.

★

Of course I did contact Glenn Miller, Jimmy Priddy, and all the others who had helped make my New York stay so memorable when I got back to England. I kept in touch with Jimmy until he died many years later in Los Angeles. Only a few of those great musicians are alive today, but I have made sure, over the years, that they know they will never be forgotten, both musically and as perhaps the greatest and most generous gentlemen I have ever met.

A FORD MODEL T ALLOWED US
TO MEET SOMEONE SPECIAL

With my New York vacation over, I got down seriously to becoming a pilot in the Royal Air Force. Finally, early in 1944, I graduated at 34 SFTS in Medicine Hat, Alberta, proudly wore my wings, and did what I had to do in the RAF. But if you've been waiting to hear about my flying career, I plan to disappoint you.

I have never been very warlike in my attitude toward people of any nation. I went to school at Buxton College, where we had more than twenty German students. In the circus, there were people from many countries. As long as the people I meet behave, I couldn't care less what country they come from. The Second World War was supposed to end all wars. Obviously, looking around today, it did not succeed. But before I get away from those war years in Canada, I would like to flash back to my time at 32 Elementary Flying School (EFS) in Bowden, Alberta. I had not then met Peter Middleton and had no idea of the adventures that lay ahead, but I think you will enjoy two stories from my stay there.

★

Good luck must have taken me to No. 32, about halfway between Calgary and Edmonton, as there were more than a dozen other EFTS stations in Canada where I could have trained. The people in Bowden and nearby Innisfail and Red Deer treated us like kings. One farmer, John Ramey, and his family chose Harold "Hefty" Hetherington—a fellow trainee from Consett, County Durham in Northern England—and me to be their weekend guests for hayrides, dinners, horseback riding, and general relaxation. They astonished us by generously giving us their old Ford Model T because they had just purchased a new car.

The Model T wasn't in the best condition, but it was still running. (Dare I say now that neither of us ever had a driver's license?) It was the first car either of us had ever owned. Fortunately, Hefty was a good mechanic, and when we arrived back at camp, he and some of our RAF mechanics started work on the engine. I got rid of the rust and painted our new vehicle a beautiful sky blue. This was unique, because in 1943 you could buy any colour of car as long as it was a shade of black. We would definitely stand out on the highway.

After a couple weeks, we decided the car was in good enough shape to tackle the 130 kilometres to Calgary. We were allowed only a small ration of gasoline in those war years, so we bought a few old jerry cans for a couple dollars, and with the help of Dave MacMillan, one of the ground crew, we filled them up with the fuel we were using in our planes. Of course, this theft of fuel was strictly illegal.

The octane of the plane fuel was far less than the lowest used in today's cars, but when used in a motor vehicle of that era, it left a trail of black exhaust for about a kilometre. Sixteen kilometres from Bowden, we put our first can of illegal fuel in the tank. Sure enough, the exhaust hung high in the air behind us like a massive cat's tail. But we were far enough from the airfield for the exhaust to be seen, and all went well until we passed through the town of Olds, some fifty kilometres north of Calgary.

We were running very smoothly, if a trifle noisily, when the driver of a car that had obviously broken down on the highway waved us down. We stopped to see what help we could offer.

"You can give me a ride into Calgary, if you don't mind," said the driver.

We happily agreed and he said he would have someone come out from the city to repair or tow his car.

"Rented it," he said. "Can't rely on most wartime cars. You boys have good sense: you're driving a Ford. But I don't think you are doing the engine any good using that airplane fuel. You'll burn it out in less than five hundred miles."

We explained the small gas allocation we were allowed and even admitted to rather illegally obtaining the plane fuel. We chatted about the war, England, and where we hoped to go in our Model T. As we approached Calgary, we asked where our guest wished to be dropped.

"At the Palliser Hotel," he answered. "If you're going in that direction."

We were. The Palliser was the most luxurious hotel in Calgary, and we explained that we were to stay right across the street for two nights at the three-dollar-a-night York Hotel, which was spotlessly clean but not quite as deluxe as the Palliser.

He asked our names and gave us a business card from his wallet. We didn't read it until we settled into our hotel room. Our eyes opened wide when we saw the name: *Edsel Ford, President, Ford Motor Company Inc., Detroit, Michigan.* We were somewhat startled. Could this be some relative of the legendary Henry Ford who had launched the Ford Company?

We were considering this when the room phone rang. It was Edsel Ford.

"I would like to thank you boys for your help today," he said, "Would you care to join me at the Palliser this evening? I'll reserve a table for three for dinner."

Of course we went. We had a delightful evening and didn't get back to the York until after midnight. We enjoyed ourselves so much, we never did get to ask Edsel Ford—who we then knew was indeed Henry Ford's son—why he had not been driving a Ford when we found him stranded on the highway or what could possibly have brought him to Canada from Detroit.

When it was time to check out of the York two days later, we went to the desk to pay our bill. "No bill," said the clerk. "Mr. Ford paid it. And he asked me to give you these two envelopes." When we opened them, we found inside each one a brand new one hundred dollar bill. We had never seen one of those before.

We called the Palliser to express our thanks, but Mr. Ford had left the day before. We climbed into our Model T and drove back to Bowden. We filled our tank fifty kilometres from the camp with our last can of regular gasoline and drove through the gates with no telltale plume of exhaust hanging behind us.

That should have been the happy ending to the story, but it wasn't.

★

Four days after we had resumed flying the delightful new single-wing Cornell plane that our course had introduced into Canada, Harold and I were called to the office of the base commanding officer. A little fearful that our theft of RAF gasoline had been discovered, we were delighted to find ourselves greeted by a big smile.

"I had a rather unexpected telephone call about an hour ago," said the commanding officer. "A Mr. Edsel Ford, who apparently is the president of the Ford Motor Company in Detroit, called me from Michigan. He requested permission for a Ford Company plane to land on our airfield tomorrow morning.

"He told me you were able to do him a service this past weekend when his car had broken down on the highway, and he wishes to do something in return. Now don't ask me what it is, because he didn't explain, and since calls from the president of the Ford Company don't come my way every day, I didn't ask. Of course, I granted permission for the plane to land, and I will reorganize your day's activities for tomorrow so you can be free to meet whoever arrives in the plane."

At ten o'clock the next morning, a plane clearly marked with the insignia of the Ford Motor Company came down smoothly on our one runway and taxied over to the main hangar. Hefty and I were ushered over by RAF police to greet the pilot and its two passengers: two men dressed in overalls. The commanding officer himself came out to greet them, and to give the moment a memorable touch, the station bugler greeted them with a fanfare that was mostly in tune.

Everyone shook hands and we were escorted into the officers' mess for a cup of tea. The two mechanics then brought out a dozen boxes of equipment, which they loaded on a trolley and took to the parking lot on the base, where the world's only existing light-blue Ford Model T stood in state. Tony and Edmund, the mechanics, got to work. Hefty and I watched as they just about rebuilt the entire mechanical operation of the vehicle. They wouldn't stop for lunch, and five hours later, after a few runs on the highway, they declared themselves satisfied, shook hands with Hefty and I, and told their pilot to prepare for takeoff.

"You won't have to worry about this baby for years," said Tony. He then whispered, "And should you find it necessary to use airplane fuel, we guarantee there will be no cat's tail hanging in the air behind the car." They also left behind five large cans of legal fuel.

We invited the mechanics to join us for a meal in the base cafeteria, but they declined, saying they had to be on their way back to Detroit as fast as possible. It was then I summoned enough courage to ask why Edsel Ford had not been driving a Ford when we found him stranded on the highway.

Tony laughed. "Mr. Ford is an intelligent man," he said. "Today's rental cars are far from reliable. Imagine the stories if the Ford president had been found stranded on a highway beside a broken-down Ford! He never drives a Ford when he is more than a hundred miles from Detroit."

From that day on, our Ford Model T purred like a kitten. Of course we wrote to Edsel Ford, thanking him for his generosity, but we never did receive a reply. I learned many years later that shortly after his visit to Calgary he had taken ill, and he died from cancer in 1943. Many years later I learned from a reliable source at the Ford Company that Edsel Ford had been on a private visit to Calgary to talk with a doctor he hoped might have discovered a cure for cancer.

Hefty and I used our souped-up Ford Model T to travel all over Alberta, including a long drive up the Alaskan Highway north of Edmonton. It never once let us down. Along the highway, we picked up dozens of hitchhikers and people standing beside broken-down cars, but we never did meet another Edsel Ford.

When we left Bowden to move on to an advanced training school, we gave the car to Dave MacMillan, who had continued to keep us well supplied with airplane fuel during our stay at 32 EFTS. I was told later that he used it to take his Canadian bride from nearby Red Deer on their honeymoon at Chateau Lake Louise, in the beautiful Rocky Mountains. A fitting use for a great car.

Thank you, John Ramey, for making this memory possible by your generous gift of the Model T; and Tony, Edmund, and Dave, we will never forget you. Wherever you are, Edsel Ford, you will surely know that you enhanced the lives of two unimportant but very grateful young RAFers. Thanks to your gesture, I have bought and enjoyed many Ford cars over the years.

20

I STOLE WINSTON CHURCHILL'S FLAG

My flying days with the British Royal Air Force came to an end in late 1944, due to delayed medical reasons that followed my bout with rheumatic fever. I made a decision to join many other grounded flyers and volunteered to go down into the coal mines, where workers were desperately needed. At the mine in Doncaster, Yorkshire, in northern England, I had the good fortune to meet a young British actor who I am still in touch with sixty-nine years later.

Brian Rix had been with the White Rose Players in Harrogate until he volunteered to join the RAF; but like me, he ended his flying career by learning how tough it was to become a coal miner. After the war, Brian went on to great success. He directed and appeared in many plays and became the owner of the Whitehall Theatre in London, home of many wonderful plays like *Dry Rot, Reluctant Heroes*, and *Simple Spyman*, among others, which earned him the name, "King of the Farce."

He achieved fame and wealth making films and starring on television, but he didn't hoard or waste his money. As an avid worker for Mencap, the British association devoted to helping those with learning disabilities, he gave and raised millions of pounds. Eventually he became chairman of Mencap and—unpaid as always—he still is today. His eldest daughter, Shelley (who sadly died two years ago), was born with Downs syndrome, and it was her struggles that made him the generous and giving man he has been all his life. Brian and his wife, Elspet, moved in 2011 to a new home in Surrey to be near their other daughter.

Brian Rix received a CBE (Commander of the British Empire) in 1977 and a knighthood in 1986, and in 1992 he was elevated to the peerage and is now Lord Rix of Whitehall. I hear from him every Christmas. (In 2012 he told me Elspet had a major medical problem but was fighting it well. So it was a very disturbing shock when I discovered that she died in late February 2013. It was the end of what must surely have been the most loving marriage in the world of show business.) We often talk about cricket, a sport we both love. But I must admit, Brian was a much better player than me. I discovered from the original scorecard he sent me this past year that he once played at the hallowed Lords Cricket Ground. The nearest I got to that achievement was sitting in the stands as a spectator.

Sadly, I just wasn't healthy enough to handle the tough life the miners endured underground. When doctors decided I had no future there, I quite expected (although the war was not yet over) to be given my walking papers from the RAF and sent back to civilian life. So it was somewhat of a shock to find myself assigned, without any explanation, to RAF headquarters in London.

I had no idea what my duties would be and was astonished—only an hour after being shown to the small bedroom that was to be my home—to be escorted to a boardroom, where I found myself facing nine military bigwigs from all three branches of the service. I answered every one of the questions they threw at me as honestly as I could, but was told I could ask no questions myself. The interrogation lasted more than an hour. Finally, one high-ranking RAF officer stood up and addressed me. "Foster," he said, "we thank you for attending this rather unusual board. If the questions seemed at times personal, we intended them to be that way."

He looked at the other officers and they all nodded to him.

"You have satisfied us that you are worthy of the job you are to be given," he said. "You will return to your quarters now and in a few days will be given your instructions. Dismiss."

I saluted him and the board, and left the room. What had I gotten myself into? I had no idea; and frankly, I was more than a little scared. I needed help, so I called my Uncle Tommy (Sir Thomas Beecham), who lived in London. Uncle Tommy, the renowned conductor of the London Philharmonic Orchestra, was the man who had helped me run away from Buxton College eight years earlier, at just thirteen, to join a circus. I had turned to him many times when I needed an answer to something difficult. I hoped he was influential enough to find out what the RAF had in store for me.

Uncle Tommy told me to get a taxi to his home. The first thing I noticed on arrival was that his eyes were twinkling. From experience, I knew this only happened when he was pleased about something he had done and was in possession of a major secret he might or might not be prepared to reveal.

"Did you pass?" he demanded even before I was inside the front door.

"Pass what?" I countered

"The bloody inquisition. Did they approve you?"

"Isn't it time you told me what this is all about?"

"Then you don't know yet?"

"Know what?"

"That you are to serve the next six months under the direct control of my dear friend, Prime Minister Winston Churchill."

"OK. Tell me, what you have done?"

"Nothing, really. I merely talked with Winston and told him you were no longer fit enough to fly, and the coal mines had turned you down, and you needed an important job where you could serve your country. He agreed to see what he could do. Sorry about what they put you through but the top brass don't know you as I do and they had to be sure."

"Sure about what?"

"Sure you could be given a secret that few people in England know. I know, because Winston trusts me, but I've never been there myself. Doubt if they would let me in anyway."

"What's the secret? Where am I going?"

"If I told you I would probably be locked up in the Tower of London, and I'm not sure they aren't still beheading people who blab about things that are secret. You'll find out when they are ready to tell you."

He flatly refused to say another word, except that I would know everything when the time was right.

A week after the interview, I was told one morning to climb aboard an official-looking car standing outside RAF headquarters.

"Don't take anything with you," said the wing commander who had been dealing with me. "You will be coming back here most nights to sleep."

That was a little comforting. At least I wasn't going to be dropped by parachute into Germany. Although, I thought I could use my knowledge of the German language I had picked up during my brief stay at Buxton College. (Yes, believe it or not, that dumb thought actually entered my mind.)

We drove for just seven minutes before pulling up beside a very nondescript entrance to a low building just a hundred yards away from London's impressive parliament buildings. My driver went ahead toward a doorway that entered into a single-storey building. The only thing that brightened the drab London day was a Union Jack flying proudly above the doorway, slapping in the breeze against dozens of sandbags that topped the roof of the structure.

Inside the door was a security room. I was checked much more thoroughly than you would experience today during an airport pat down. Prints of my fingerprints were taken and they took at least half a dozen photographs of me from every possible angle. At least I was allowed to keep my clothes on.

Then the questions began. I had to give my mother's maiden name, where my father was born, and my addresses in England in three different communities–even the name of a lady who had once been my next-door neighbour.

How they knew about Eileen O'Neill, who lived at 51 Mersey Road in Heaton Mersey, I will never know. But she had once been a renowned opera singer and had sung with Paul Robeson. They seemed delighted I could recall her dog's name.

Then I was finally allowed to enter what I was told for the first time were the British government's top-secret Cabinet War Rooms.

"When you leave each day, you will forget this bunker exists," said an officer. "You will not at any time remove or attempt to remove any documents from any of the War Rooms. You will obey without question every order given to you by any officer, and only Prime Minister Winston Churchill can countermand those orders."

It was a week before I met Mr. Churchill. My workweek was often seven days—and nights too. I stayed overnight and had a bed in a small room where I kept a towel and my toothbrush and toothpaste, plus a change of clothes. I was told I could wear civilian clothes if I wished, but I never did. I think I was too proud of my uniform.

On several occasions during the first few weeks, I recall being talked to by strangers in restaurants and other places outside the bunker. I was still wearing my wings, of course, and I simply told people I was now grounded and doing clerical work at RAF headquarters. It wasn't long before I realized the strangers were planted to see if I could keep my mouth shut about the War Rooms. Nobody ever officially confirmed that, but the encounters with strangers were too frequent to be anything else.

★

After a while, it became usual to see the prime minister in his office, which adjoined a simple bedroom, or in the cabinet room of the bunker. I recognized a lot of other important people too. Prime Minister Churchill rarely stayed overnight. I was told he preferred his bedroom at 10 Downing Street. Incredible as it may seem in this age of armed security and entourages, the great man actually walked home alone late at night. I know that for a fact, because I saw him make the walk—although I was reprimanded the next day for actually following him home.

I worked there for almost nine months before I was told my demobilization papers had come through and I was again to become a civilian.

Don't ask me to tell you what I did in the bunker or what I saw

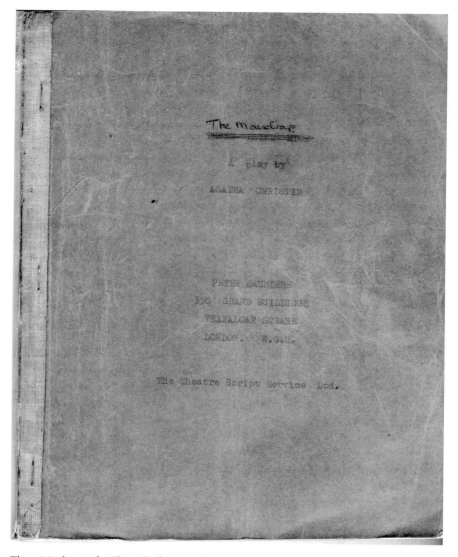

The Mousetrap

A play by

AGATHA CHRISTIE

PETER SAUNDERS
350 GRAND BUILDINGS
TRAFALGAR SQUARE
LONDON. W.C.2.

The Theatre Script Service Ltd.

The original script for *Three Blind Mice*, a play written by Agatha Christie, which became *The Mousetrap*.

Frank Sinatra was at the height of his fame in 1943 when he gave me this autographed photograph. We remained friends throughout his illustrious life, and I looked after his publicity when he appeared in England after the Second World War.

In 1958 I was able to repay drummer Cozy Cole for his kindness in New York in 1943 by making his record *Topsy* a bestseller worldwide. He visited the CKEY Radio station in Toronto with superb jazz organist Earl Grant. Joe Crysdale (far left) was our sports announcer; he taught me that baseball was more fun that cricket.

While I represented Richard Burton and Elizabeth Taylor, I arranged for them to attend many functions for publicity photographs. Here they are with Michael Redgrave and Princess Margaret in London.

The man on the left was Harold Jenkins when he came to my office at CKEY Radio in Toronto in 1958. When he left, he was Conway Twitty and had a contract for his first hit record: *It's Only Make Believe*.

They say to never approach a wild bear if you accidentally encounter one in your travels. I didn't know this rule when I met this friendly bear in Banff, Alberta, in 1943. Harold Hetherington, my RAF pal, used my two-dollar Kodak box camera to record this special moment in my life.

Among the word-renowned big band leaders I was fortunate to meet in New York City on leave in 1943 was—perhaps the most famous Canadian-born leader of all time—Guy Lombardo. In 1959 I was privileged to present a concert with his orchestra in Toronto, which raised funds for the area's animal centre.

I was only thirteen when I saw Jesse Owens win four gold medals at the 1936 Berlin Olympics. This picture was taken when we met again in London after the war, when I had the privilege of helping to publicize a visit he made to England and, again, Berlin.

One of my most pleasant memories from Hollywood in 1943 was meeting Shirley Temple. We became good friends. She used to phone me at the RAF base in Canada, where I returned after my leave. For several years she wrote me at least once a month. We never did meet again.

The entrance to the two suites in the bungalow at Hearst Castle, where Charlie Chaplin and I stayed during our 1943 visit.

This photograph was printed in newspapers around the world—in many cases on the front page—in 1957. It told a story we cooked up in Switzerland to help promote Woburn Abbey, ancestral home of the Duke of Bedford. This is the official "group rescue" picture, which I took. From the left, producer Billy Boyle, who had supposedly been out looking for the lost group; film makeup artist Harry Claff; Swiss rescuer Hans Eggar; Elaine Stewart, star of the film *High Hell*, which we were making; and Ian, the Duke of Bedford. Ian told me months later that he had clippings of the "rescue" from over two hundred daily newspapers and magazines.

My wife, Irene, and I on our wedding day: August 14, 1948. She has survived being married to me now for sixty-five years, and we are still enjoying a good life.

Sidney Olcott, Canadian-born silent film director, opened his home to me in Hollywood in 1943. Photographs I took of Sid and his wife, Val, have vanished, but I still have this one, which he gave me, from the days when he was, according to Charlie Chaplin, the number one film director in the world.

On leave in Hollywood during the Second World War in 1943, it was my delight to meet the great Canadian actress Mary Pickford, known as the Queen of Hollywood. For more than twenty years after our meeting, we remained friends. At Christmas I always received a family greeting. This one, from 1948, shows Mary (Mrs. Buddy Rogers), her husband, Buddy, children, Ronnie and Roxanne, and the family dog, Butch.

Pictured here are three of the great Glenn Miller wartime band members who remained friends of mine for life (from left to right): trombonist Jimmy Priddy, bassist Trigger Alpert, and drummer Ray McKinley. They kept in touch for many years and visited my parents' home in England as well as my postwar home in Toronto.

Many top Hollywood and New York stars were, like me, in uniform when I met them in 1943. Actor/singer Tony Martin (far left) joined me, band leader Glenn Miller (second from right), and actor Broderick Crawford (far right) at the CBS Radio studio where they were recording a special show for the American Armed Forces.

The most renowned big band leader in the world during the Second World War was Glenn Miller. He and I became good friends and spent many hours in New York discussing plans for his band to fly to England to entertain the troops—including a private concert on the lawn of my parents' home near Manchester.

The Duke of Bedford was a down-to-earth British peer who needed to promote his ancestral home to tourists in England. Here, he and I are pictured on top of the Jungfrau Mountain in Switzerland, where he agreed to get "lost in a blizzard" as a major publicity stunt during the filming of the appropriately titled film, *High Hell*, in 1957.

As a member of the Royal Air Force on leave in New York in 1943, I was introduced to everyone I wanted to meet in the musical world. The man who made it all possible was trumpeter and bandleader Russ Case (at rear). Two of his good friends were singer Georgia Gibbs (centre) and NBC studio bandleader Jimmy Lytell (right).

Jimmy Edwards (lower left) and Benny Hill (top right) were guests of my wife Irene and I at a banquet in London in the 1950s. I met Jimmy while in the RAF in Moncton and Benny on Central Pier in Blackpool, England, where he was beginning his fabulous career in 1952.

and learned, because the secrecy document I signed is, I understand, still officially operative. What they would do to me, I have no idea—but I plan to take no chances. I don't believe the Tower of London or beheading is now among the penalties, but who knows what action could be taken.

One of the most pleasant happenings in the bunker was meeting, two days after my arrival, with Margaret Brooks. Margaret and I were old friends. Before the war started, we used to travel on the same train to Manchester every day, where I was working with my father at his business, and Margaret and I often went out to the theatre at night.

Before I joined the RAF, Margaret, a year older than me, had already joined the Women's Auxiliary Air Force. Before I came to Canada for my flight training I received a letter from her telling me she had been assigned to Bletchley, the top-secret centre near London, where the decoding of military secrets was a major success story of the Second World War. Her work there brought her to the Cabinet War Rooms, and her presence every day made my stay very enjoyable.

Every morning, I saw the Union Jack that flew outside the cabinet rooms raised. Every night, I saw it ceremoniously lowered before being carefully put away in the security office inside the bunker. Since I could take nothing from the bunker itself, I decided I wanted that flag as a souvenir of a time in my life I knew I would never forget.

So just before dusk, three days before I was due to leave the bunker for the final time—with the aid of Margaret Brooks, who delayed him—I beat the corporal to the flag by about ten minutes, hauled it to the ground, and took off with it to my room at RAF headquarters.

The next morning, a new flag was in place on a brand new pole, which had a safety device attached to stop anyone else from copying my thievery. But not a word was spoken about the old flag having vanished.

On my final day in the bunker, I was called into the prime minister's room. Churchill put out his hand, thanked me for my work, and wished me luck in the years ahead.

I saluted and turned away.

"Oh," he said. "There is one more thing. Since you already have my flag, perhaps you would care to have the flagpole as well."

From the side of his desk, he produced the short flagpole and handed it over to me with a huge smile. I was too stunned to respond, but I could hear him chuckling as I left the room.

I don't know what happened to the flagpole—it might have got lost when I came across the Atlantic to make North America my home—but I still have the flag in a drawer in my basement. Now and again, I take it out and hang it in my workroom for a few hours so I will never forget a momentous time in my life. I was offered a lot of money for my purloined flag a few years ago, but I can't imagine ever selling such a wonderful souvenir of the terrible war we thought would end all wars.

Perhaps I should be trying to find a suitable home for this memory of the nine months of my life that I shall never be able to write about, although what I would have to say might astonish a lot of people and give well-deserved credit to a lot of unsung heroes, including Margaret Brooks, who did more to help end the war than will ever be known.

MY FINAL WEEKEND LEAVE
FROM THE RAF

Before the war, when I came home from the Fossett's Circus, I had spent many happy hours at the Theatre Royal in Stockport. It was not a number-one theatre, but many of the radio stars of that era headlined the weekly variety shows and revues.

The theatre's stage manager, Joe Cartwright, gave me a job as an unpaid stagehand, so I met most of them. Included among those acquaintances was a little eight-year-old girl who was there with her stepfather and mother, Ted and Barbara Andrews, a popular radio and music hall act.

Barbara asked me to babysit their daughter in the dressing room while they were onstage. The girl had apparently wandered onstage occasionally when they were doing their act, and they wanted to keep her occupied and quiet.

But as I listened to the youngster singing in the dressing room each night, I realized she had a remarkable voice. It was really easy to convince her parents to let her go onstage and join their act for one song. I believe that was the youngster's first official public appearance as a singer. She was not a star then—but of course you all know what happened to Julie Andrews in the years that followed.

When I arrived home early one Saturday on my final leave before being released from the RAF, I could think of no better place to go for the evening than the Theatre Royal, where I could say hello again to the man who had helped me before the war: Joe Cartwright.

It was a great decision; and to this day, I have a framed poster on the wall of the entrance lobby at my home in Riverview, New Brunswick, from the show that was appearing there for the Christmas season.

Before I joined the RAF, I had the same seat in the front row—A13, near the string section of the orchestra—at every show the theatre presented. When I learned that Joe Cartwright was still stage manager, I called him at his home to ask if there was any way he could get me my regular seat in the front row to see *Robinson Crusoe*, the pantomime due to open that night.

Joe told me every seat was sold, but he was delighted I was home and felt sure he could convince the theatre owner, Charlie Revill, to move someone out of A13 for the 6:15 P.M. show. To this day, I don't know how that miracle was achieved, or who got bumped, but when I arrived at the theatre my A13 ticket was waiting.

I was still in my RAF uniform, proudly displaying my wings. The orchestra members, whom I had known for many years, were alerted by Joe, and gave me a round of applause as I took the seat I had occupied so many times.

For those who don't know, a British pantomime is a musical version of one of the many wonderful stories—like *Cinderella, Jack and the Beanstalk*, and *Aladdin*—that we all enjoyed as kids. All these shows had principal boys and girls; the lead characters, both played by female actors, a male comedian who played the role of a woman (the Dame), and most importantly, a line of dancers who were always young and beautiful.

This show—*Robinson Crusoe*, starring the great comic Arthur White—was no different. But it had one dancer, also playing the role of the good fairy, who was not simply beautiful, but gorgeous. At the end of the first act, I recall going over to Snowy, the orchestra drummer, and asking, "Did you see that girl? Snowy, she's for me!"

When the curtain came down at the end of the first of the two evening performances, I headed backstage through the pass door and told Joe Cartwright I had to meet this lovely girl. The program said her name was Irene Dodds. Joe took me to the dancers' dressing room and told Irene a special friend of his wanted to meet her. I spent the entire two hours of the second performance that night backstage, talking to Irene every second she was not performing.

With Joe's approval—happily for me, he told Irene I was respectable—I was allowed, after the second show, to walk her home from the theatre to the boarding house where she and the other dancers were staying for two weeks. We stopped at a fish-and-chip shop on the way and I spent about six pence buying a snack for the two of us as we walked home.

The show, which was staged three times a day, was at the Theatre Royal for two weeks; we met every day of the first week before I had to go back to base. Irene even came to my parents' home in nearby Heaton Mersey for many meals between the afternoon and evening shows.

Irene and I never lost touch, and even though she was a wonderful dancer and quickly moved to bigger shows in the best theatres around England, I was able, after a year, to convince her to marry me and give up her dreams of stardom in the theatre.

Life for us wasn't always easy. We had little money at first, but managed to raise our two children, Beverley and Ian, in the way we wish kids were raised today.

We moved to London before coming to the United States and Canada and have over the years travelled on vacations to South America, North Africa, Europe, Hong Kong, Bali, Bangkok, and Singapore. I checked recently and discovered that we have visited twenty-eight different countries around the world.

We have driven right across the United States and Canada by car, and have made many trips to New York to see the wonderful live shows that city has to offer.

In 1970 we came to Riverview, New Brunswick, for what was intended to be a six-week stay to help out the publisher of the *Moncton Free Press,* a weekly newspaper whose editor had died suddenly. I remembered the friendliness of Moncton from the war years when I first stepped foot on Canadian soil in 1943, and found very little had changed, so after a year we bought the house we had rented, and have stayed here to this day. It was the best move of our lives. This surely has to be the best part of any country in the world.

On return visits to England we always went to the Theatre Royal to see whatever show was appearing there. Sadly, it was pulled down about twenty-five years ago and in its place now stands a supermarket.

Irene has, for some inexplicable reason, managed to survive being married to me for sixty-five years now. We have lots of happy memories and we laugh a lot. I think she will agree I am telling the truth when I say that she, too, is still enjoying a wonderful life.

Our son and daughter have both been successful in their work and marriages and have blessed us with four grandchildren, and we recently celebrated the arrival of our second great granddaughter.

By the time we were married, I was back in civilian life. My father, who ran a successful company, thought I would join him there, but his business just wasn't for me. With Irene's blessing, we took a gamble and moved to London, where I hoped to use all the contacts I had made with people in the world of entertainment.

With no experience at all, I became an entertainment publicist. As you will discover, I didn't do too badly at all in my chosen profession, and both our lives have benefitted from the great people who populate the most satisfying industry in the world: show business.

THE DAY RICHARD BURTON REFUSED TO DIE

Actor Richard (Dick) Burton was just starting his illustrious career when the incident I am about to relate took place. The eminent British comedian Jimmy Edwards, Richard Burton (who had served with me in the RAF) and I met regularly at the Captain's Cabin, a pub on Norris Street, just off Piccadilly in London's West End.

I had by then become a show business publicist in a small way and was managing to earn a living.

Jimmy was already establishing himself, playing the starring comedy role at London's Windmill Theatre, where he often admitted nobody knew his name because everyone in the audience was there to do one thing: gaze at the thirty gorgeous girls who danced onstage every night in the skimpiest costumes allowed by law.

I had managed to get his picture in a couple papers—with the girls of course—and I think he paid me about five pounds for this achievement. But he had a long way to go to reach ultimate stardom on radio, stage, and television.

One day we had a special reason to celebrate: Dick had just secured a role in a period play called *Much Ado About Everything*, a parody on the Shakespearean play of a similar name. The role had immense potential to enhance Dick's career, because the renowned actor Laurence Olivier had agreed to direct. Olivier was already distinguished for his superb dramatic abilities, but this was, as far as I know, his first shot at directing.

Jimmy and I spent many hours with Dick each day, rehearsing every line until we were convinced he would undoubtedly make a major impression onstage. On opening night, Jimmy and I were permitted to stand in the wings just offstage. We knew that at the end of act one, Dick had to pick up a small glass, supposedly full of poison, from an upstage table. He then had to speak these words from the script: "I shall drink this…" (*raise glass and drink potion with face contorted in agony*), "and die!" This parody from another Shakespearean play suited our plan to perfection: Jimmy and I felt we might be able to enhance the scene.

We collected the glass, full of cold tea, from the prop table at the side of the stage, where it stood until it was ready to be carried onstage to end the act. We took the glass into the men's washroom, poured out the tea, and refilled it with…surely you can guess.

The play, which really wasn't very good, went amazingly well. Dick received several spontaneous bursts of applause for an outstanding performance. As rehearsed, at the end of act one, he picked up the glass and turned to the fair lady for whom he was about to die.

"I shall drink this…" he said in the magnificent voice that later conquered the world's stages and screens. He downed the liquid and spluttered out the words, "and die." With a very red face, he then turned to the audience and spoke directly to them. "But first, I'll kill the bastards who peed in my potion."

He unsheathed his sword and headed directly for Jimmy and me. Fortunately for us a small piece of scenery broke off when his swinging sword impaled it, preventing his assassination attempt from becoming reality. His red face turned white. Realizing what he had done, he said, "Oh, my God!" With the chunk of scenery still firmly attached to his sword, he turned around and strode back onstage with all the dignity he could muster.

He bowed to the audience. "The varlets are dead," he said. To the unfortunate actress who had been left onstage wondering what on earth to do next, he added, "And now I shall die."

He collapsed onstage as the intermission curtain came down.

Laurence Olivier came backstage through the pass door from the audience as Dick got to his feet and walked into the wings.

"Richard," said Olivier harshly, "there is something you need to know. When I create a scene it must be played exactly as directed. My instructions are supposed to be engraved inside your head. The lines must not be altered, no matter what calamity befalls you."

Dick, expecting to be fired on the spot, hung his head. "Yes, Mr. Olivier," he said in a very subdued voice. "It will never happen again."

Suddenly Olivier began roaring with laughter. "More's the pity Richard," he said. "It was so bloody funny that I peed my pants."

"Better than in my potion," said Dick.

Olivier and Dick left the stage together, arm in arm. Jimmy and I got out of the theatre fast.

It was a week before I heard from Dick again. When he called, I was surprised at the friendly tone in his voice. "Let's meet for lunch," he said. "Call Jimmy and ask him to join us." Understandably, we both anticipated the worst. We were quite sure that he had something diabolical in store for us.

But he greeted us at the restaurant with a huge grin on his face.

"I want you to know that what happened the other night is forgiven. Olivier told the story to a lot of important people, and suddenly I found directors and producers banging on my door offering me good roles onstage and in films. It was the best thing that ever happened to me."

Decades later, he told me he believed his successful career began that awful opening night of *Much Ado About Everything*. "It was a revolting way to start," he said, "but even today people remind me of it, and the potion doesn't taste quite so evil now."

THE TAMING OF THE BOLSHOI BALLET IN LONDON

By 1950 my publicity office was doing very well. I had some good clients who had money to pay me, and when the Red Army Chorus arrived in London direct from Moscow for their first overseas tour, I was chosen, for some unknown reason, to handle the publicity for the group. I never found out why I was selected for this honour, but the army singers turned out to be great guys. Whatever I asked, they did. Some had even taken the trouble to learn to speak English, and when, at my suggestion, they concluded each performance by singing *"Auld Lang Syne,"* the audience rose to its feet applauding and cheering.

The positive publicity the group got in the press, on the radio, and in the early television shows was more than anyone, including the Russian embassy, had hoped for. And so two years later, when it was announced by the embassy that the famed Bolshoi Ballet from Moscow would be making its first appearance outside of Russia at London's Royal Opera House in Covent Garden, I wasn't surprised when I was called to see the Russian ambassador and asked to handle the show's publicity. He shook my hand and said they were sure I would do as good a job with the ballet as I had with the Red Army Chorus.

Little did we all know it wasn't going to be like that at all.

★

Every daily paper in London, plus radio and TV networks—and even some papers as far away as Australia and most European capitals—notified my office that they wanted to talk to the dancers. It looked as though I had another winner on my hands. But when I approached the tour manager, Igor Volkov, through an interpreter to ask if photographers could attend the first rehearsal in London, I was met with a very definite *nyet*. *Nyet* after *nyet* followed. The press would not be allowed to talk to any of the dancers, nor would they be allowed to attend rehearsals, and no cameras were to be allowed backstage or anywhere else in the theatre at any time.

Telling the news media that they would not have any access to the ballet company didn't help my reputation as a publicist at all. In fact, one renowned entertainment writer publicly stated that he would never again mention any of my clients in his column unless he was allowed to interview the Bolshoi's star dancers.

Then along came Sydney Bourne. Known as the "Bearded Budget Couturier," he made attractive women's dresses at remarkably low prices. Sydney, for whom I had completed a successful publicity campaign a year earlier, suggested I propose to the tour manager that all of the dancers visit his showroom, with each dancer allowed to take away any two dresses she wished, free of charge.

The tour manager responded to this request with one more *nyet*. Then I had a bright idea. Would the proposed idea be considered if perhaps the manager himself could take home three dresses for his wife back in Moscow?

"*Nyet*," he said. Then he actually smiled and added something else in Russian.

The translator explained: "Mr. Volkov says not three, but six dresses for his wife, and the deal will be approved. But no news media may be allowed to attend the occasion."

Sydney Bourne nodded his head. He asked for a picture of Volkov's wife so he might make the appropriate size especially for her. She turned out to be a heavyweight, but Bourne said he would have the dresses made on time for the visit to his showroom. We settled on a date only four days ahead, but Sydney said the Volkov dresses would be ready.

When the day came for the principals and corps de ballet to visit the showroom, they were picked up by a bus at the back entrance of their hotel and driven there quietly.

The excited dancers romped through the showroom and selected not two dresses each, but as many as they could carry. David Sim, my photographer, was not supposed to be there; but since Mr. Volkov was not with the group we decided he might get a few good pictures that we could somehow use. We didn't know how good the pictures would turn out to be.

The dainty little dancers got into fist fights over the dresses and several were rolling all over the floor grabbing at other dancers and their dresses. The twenty dancers just about stripped the Bourne showroom bare. Between them they took almost two hundred dresses. Although Sydney had hired two translators, they were totally unable to convince the happy dancers that "two" had not meant "ten."

The next day, David Sim showed me the pictures he had taken. Most were excellent and deserved to be given to the press. But when shown a set (not including the fights), Mr. Volkov, who had received his six specially made dresses, said *nyet* once again.

I had one more idea, which wouldn't endear me to Mr. Volkov or the Russian embassy, but might possibly get approval for the hungry press to talk with the dancers.

I showed Volkov copies of the fight pictures and said that unless the dancers and rehearsals were made available to the media, I was going to resign my job as publicist and issue them to every paper and magazine in the world. Volkov tore them up and threw them on the ground. But his *nyet* didn't sound as convincing as it had in the past.

An hour later I was called to the Russian embassy. There, the ambassador was waiting for me, holding the torn fight pictures. He actually smiled at me.

"This is perhaps the best thing that could have happened," he said. "We wanted the dancers to talk to the press, but the Bolshoi said no. Now, if you will promise to destroy all the fight negatives, the dancers will be made available."

I had all the other good pictures from the Bourne showroom with me for him to see. He picked out six he liked and told me to issue them to the press.

Sydney got amazing publicity for his beautiful dresses, which were modelled by the dancers in studio pictures printed in papers worldwide, and David and I got the fight pictures as souvenirs, which we have never shown anyone, as promised. David is now gone, but I still have my photos.

Mr. Volkov was recalled to Russia, and the new tour manager, obviously alerted to the fact that very damaging pictures might be shown if he was uncooperative, opened the doors to the news media and everyone was happy.

But I never did get another assignment from the Russian embassy.

LANA TURNER SAID HE WOULD
NEVER MAKE IT IN THE MOVIES

Lana Turner was at the height of her long Hollywood career when she arrived in England in the summer of 1957 to make the Paramount film *Another Time, Another Place.* I was hired to be her publicist.

At that time, my publicity office in London was being kept busy fifteen hours a day, and handled people like Frank Sinatra, Jerry Lee Lewis, Liberace, and Bill Haley and His Comets, but I welcomed the chance to see Lana again. I had met her at MGM Studios in Hollywood in 1943, when I was on leave there from my RAF pilot training in Canada. She had been very helpful to me then, and I looked forward to returning the favour during her British visit.

When she arrived, I introduced her to just about every major British film writer. Lana never missed a photo session or an interview appointment, and it looked as though everything was going to run very smoothly. We got wonderful press coverage thanks to her co-operation.

The day after she arrived in London, Lana attended a film premiere and was introduced to a young Scottish actor who had somehow managed an invitation. The young actor enchanted Lana and she insisted on him being given a part in her film that would be the biggest so far in his career. He had only appeared previously in small roles in three British films.

Another Time, Another Place was shot at the Metro-Goldwyn-Mayer studio in North London. The young actor had a nice role as Lana's love interest who was killed in the Second World War. It was a pleasant set on which we all worked happily. Lewis Allen, the director, was a quiet man who didn't believe in shouting at actors. His calm temperament made everything easy.

The publicity we obtained on both sides of the Atlantic delighted Lana and Paramount Pictures. (Paramount had no studio in London, so the film was made at MGM.)

Barry Sullivan was the only other American in the film. The rest of the cast was chosen by Lana and Lewis Allen in England. They included Glynnis Johns, Terence Longdon, and Sidney James.

At first Lana was very happy with her young Scottish actor. But after a few weeks of shooting, she was obviously getting a little frustrated. "I can't understand you half the time," she said, "can't you try a just little harder to get rid of that Scottish accent? It is coming over far too strong."

She started to look for problems with his performance and was on the set whenever he was in a scene. Everyone was waiting for her to throw a tantrum but somehow she kept her temper in check, and two days before the end of shooting she was conspicuously absent when her "discovery" finished his last scene. When he walked over to her dressing room to say goodbye and thank her for giving him the role, she was not there.

The next day, she reappeared at the studio bright and cheerful. She took me to one side. "Do me a favour," she said. "Tell my young Scottish friend that he would be wise to get out of the film industry. Tell him with that accent, I honestly don't believe he has what it takes to become a star."

Fortunately, I decided to ignore her advice and never did tell the young actor what she had said. Which is just as well, because her "discovery" was none other than a youthful Sean Connery, who a few years later found considerable fame as James Bond and remained a major star for the rest of his highly successful career.

Happily, to this day he still has the wonderful Scottish accent that has made him the pride of the Scotland he loves so much, and which earned him the right, a year or two back, to be officially called Sir Sean Connery.

Ten years ago, when we met in New York, I finally told Sean what Lana had said! He laughed and slapped me on the back. "Do you think I proved her wrong?" he asked.

AGATHA CHRISTIE: BARTENDER AT THE AMBASSADORS

The life of mystery writer Agatha Christie was just about as mysterious as her fascinating books. She hated being photographed and rarely appeared anywhere in public. If she was seen at an event, it was only on the rare occasion when her book publisher pleaded with her to help promote her latest writings.

When I was hired by producer Peter Saunders to handle publicity on her play *The Mousetrap*, which was due to open at the Ambassadors Theatre in London in 1952, I knew nothing of her reluctance to be seen in public. I naively believed Agatha Christie's name and presence on opening night would bring us front-page headlines.

Saunders took me over to the Christie home in London. She was charming, and served us afternoon tea, but laughed uproariously when I asked where she would like to sit in the theatre on opening night.

"Charles," she said, "hasn't Peter told you I never appear in public on occasions when newsmen and photographers are likely to be present?"

I risked a question. "Mrs. Mallowan (she was married to archaeologist Max Mallowan), can I have your permission to release a story suggesting you might actually attend the play on opening night?"

She laughed. "Go ahead, if you think it will help fill the theatre, but don't expect me to be there. I'll see you at rehearsals, but no news media please." And she added, "Never call me that name again. I'm

Agatha and you are Charles from this day on."

Agatha and I became good friends. I respected her wish for privacy and never did give photographers a chance to put her where they wanted—on their front pages.

On several occasions, she quietly visited the Ambassadors Theatre when *The Mousetrap* was playing. Once, she dressed as a man and completely fooled me until she whispered in my ear, "I'm Agatha. Isn't this a great disguise?"

She often confided to me her opinion of the play. "It wasn't good enough to make a full-length book," she said. "I can't honestly believe it will survive more than one season as a play."

How wrong she and many more of us were was indelibly recorded when the play reached its sixtieth anniversary in 2012.

At the end of its second year, *The Mousetrap* had proved so popular—thanks to Richard Attenborough and his lovely wife, Sheila Sim, who were the stars of the play for its first two years—that it became the play every visitor to London wanted to see.

At the start of the third season, I had an idea that I thought might make the front pages. I suggested to Peter Saunders that we invite all the foreign ambassadors in London to the Ambassadors Theatre for a special "Ambassadors Night." I designed a specially printed, glamorous program with silk covers for the occasion. An copy, autographed by the entire cast, was to be given to each ambassador. Agatha agreed to add her signature, as long as she could do it without fuss in the privacy of her home.

We anticipated that perhaps a dozen of the forty-five ambassadors in London might accept, so we put away twenty-four seats, allowing two for each country. The rest of the theatre, as usual, sold out quickly. We were shocked when forty-three of the forty-five embassies asked for seats for their ambassadors and guests.

Just when we were wondering which ambassadors to offend by offering them seats on a less important night, something happened that I have always considered a near miracle. A phone call arrived at the box-office from a distressed lady in Manchester. She told us that her husband had died unexpectedly and wondered if it would be possible for the theatre to refund the money they had paid for the seventy seats she had reserved for their fiftieth wedding anniversary party. Incredibly, the reservations were for some of the best seats in the house on Ambassadors Night.

Peter Saunders was so relieved that he ordered me to send the grieving widow a huge floral bouquet, with a copy of the special program signed by Agatha and the cast of *The Mousetrap*. He also offered to give her six dress-circle seats free on whatever date she planned her next visit to London. Last I heard from Saunders (then elevated to Sir Peter Saunders because of the success of *The Mousetrap*), she never did take him up on his generous offer.

I told Agatha Christie that we had both the Russian and American ambassadors coming to the show. They hadn't spoken to each other in years, so she was delighted that I had placed them side by side in the front row of the dress circle.

"I've got to be there," she said. "We may have World War Three starting in the middle of the show. How can I be there without someone seeing and photographing me?"

I thought about this problem for a few days before calling Agatha.

"Do you know how to mix drinks?" I asked.

"Max will tell you I'm as good as any bartender in London," she replied.

I cemented my lifetime friendship with her that day.

"Then we'll have a special staff uniform made for you, and you can serve drinks in the private bar we are setting up at the back of the dress circle for ambassadors only," I suggested.

"I love it," she said. "There'll come a day when I can do something special for you. Just ask me." (That day did come when Italian actor Rossano Brazzi asked me to get him an invitation to visit Agatha's country home, Winterbook House, which until that day had been off limits to anyone not a family member or a personal friend. Agatha remembered her promise and Rossano was invited.)

Only Agatha Christie, Peter Saunders, and I were in on the secret. Not one ambassador recognized her. Not even the theatre staff were told who she was. She was so good at her job that the bar manager asked Peter

Saunders if he could get the new server on staff as a full-time barmaid.

The next day, Agatha told me she had listened to the American and Russian ambassadors chatting like old friends.

"I think we broke up the Cold War last night," she said. "And I made a whole pocketful of tips. When the American ambassador gave me ten shillings, the Russian doubled that and gave me a pound note."

"What did you do with all the money you made?" I asked.

"Walked around the streets and dropped the coins and notes in the boxes held in front of me by street musicians and beggars. But I didn't try to get credit for the money. I always said, 'Compliments of the American', or 'Russian,' or some other ambassador who had been generous. Those people on the street moved me so much, I plan to do that walk more often—but I won't give the ambassadors any credit in the future." She never told me if she did repeat her generosity.

My autographed copy of the special program for Ambassadors Night was stolen from my office on Shaftesbury Avenue in London several weeks later. It was never recovered, and I winced about three years ago to hear one of the programs was sold on the Internet for seventeen thousand pounds.

But I still have the original script used by Richard (now Sir Richard) Attenborough at rehearsals. It has an opening scene that was removed before the play was actually staged. And the original title printed on the cover is the title of Agatha Christie's short story *Three Blind Mice*, the inspiration for the play. That is crossed out, and *The Mousetrap* written in ink underneath. It might be worth even more than the special program.

AN UNEXPECTED MEETING WITH A KING IN ROME

Errol Flynn phoned my office one day in the mid-1950s. I soon discovered he had not forgotten the help I had given him back in 1943, when we were able to expose actor Peter Van Eyck as a German spy.

"Hi Sport," he said. "Nice to talk to you. I have good news. Right now I'm in Rome, but in a few weeks I'll be in London. Patrice [his wife] and I have signed a contract to film a television series for the American market in England. It is to be called *The Errol Flynn Theatre*, and I've seen a couple of scripts and they look promising. I want you to be the publicist on the series. Can you find time to be with me?"

Of course, I didn't hesitate. "I'll be free," I said. "When can I get details?"

"Perhaps you could fly to Rome this weekend and Patrice and I will have a lawyer here to draw up our contract," he replied. "Is that possible?"

I agreed, and the following day a call from British Overseas Airways told me I had a first-class ticket waiting for me at their office.

On my arrival in Rome, I was met at the airport by a limousine and driven to the Excelsior Hotel, where I was given a luxury suite. Errol called within minutes of my arrival to tell me he would be over for dinner that night to discuss the next day's meeting to set up our deal. We agreed to have dinner in the hotel's beautiful dining room, where the cuisine was rated among the best in the world, at seven o'clock. Errol enjoyed the subdued lighting, which allowed him to dine in peace without autograph-hunters disturbing him every few minutes.

It seemed like the perfect evening, until a waiter arrived with a verbal message for Errol. "Mr. Flynn," he said, speaking perfect English, "His Majesty would like you and your guest to join him and his guests at their table."

"His Majesty," said Flynn. "Who the heck is His Majesty?"

"His Majesty King Farouk," said the waiter.

"Farouk," said Flynn. "That Egyptian bum! He's not a king now? I didn't like him when I met him years ago in Cairo and I'm not about to move from this table to sit with him. Tell him that if he wants to talk to me he can come over here."

"Mr. Flynn," said the waiter. "King Farouk doesn't go to anyone. People go to him."

"Tell *Mr.* Farouk that I'm not 'people,'" said Flynn. "If he wants to talk to me, I'll talk to him after I have dined, but at this table."

"His Majesty won't be pleased," said the unhappy waiter, but he bowed and went away.

A minute later we heard a loud roar and looked across the dimly lit room to see Farouk getting up from his table, obviously very angry. We saw him tell the three ladies at his table to rise, and the foursome came marching (or waddling, for the rather portly Farouk) over to our table.

"Don't stand up when this bunch gets here," said Flynn. "We are the royalty here. Understand?"

I understood completely.

Farouk and three rather weather-worn ladies, who didn't look at all appealing, arrived.

Flynn glanced up. "Hello Farouk," he said. "So we meet again."

"Mr. Flynn," said Farouk in a menacing way, "when I request your presence, I expect to get your presence."

"So the unexpected happened, old chum," said Flynn. "That's always a delightful moment in life to me. Which pasture did you find these ladies in?"

I noticed a number of waiters and security guards were standing not too far away, and feared Farouk had perhaps caused disturbing incidents before in this dining room.

"Mr. Flynn, you and your guest appear to have no women with you. I suggest you come to my table and I will share with you these delectable young ladies of Rome," said Farouk.

"From the look of these specimens, I think your eyesight is fading," said Flynn. "Go back to your table, Farouk, and we will stay here. We are about to enjoy our meal, and you and your friends are not adding to the aroma around our table."

I thought for a moment that Farouk was going to hit Flynn, but as he moved forward a security guard grabbed him and led him back to his own table. His three companions followed.

"I don't deal with people like that," said Errol. "Let's enjoy our meal."

A minute later there was a major clatter from Farouk's table. We realized that he had pushed it over, scattering food, wine, and dishes everywhere. He marched out of the room, uttering remarks that even I, with no knowledge of whatever language he was using, realized were rather impolite. His three guests from the "pasture" followed, attempting to retain the dignity they'd never had.

Errol and I enjoyed our meal more than we'd ever anticipated, especially when the manager came across and thanked Errol for behaving "like a true gentleman in a very difficult situation."

He told us Farouk had twice been banned from the room because of similar incidents, and after that night would only be permitted in again if he allowed hotel security to occupy the table next to him.

The hotel notified Errol that due to his impeccable behaviour there would be no charge for my suite and should I make any purchases during my stay, they too would be complimentary. They were obviously not amused by King Farouk or his entourage.

★

You will be interested to hear that I didn't buy anything in the hotel. I took the Errol's advice. "You don't ever take advantage of moments like this," he said.

The next day at our business meeting, I met a rather attractive young lady who told me her name was Rossana Cappo. "I am coming to London with the Flynns," she said. "I understand Errol wants me to meet his son, Sean."

Rossana did come to London and for a brief while played Sean's girlfriend in a segment of the *Errol Flynn Theatre* TV series. Errol later changed her name to Rossana Rory, and she became a very successful TV and film personality in Rome. She appeared in two segments of the Errol Flynn TV series and, in 1957, Errol took her to Cuba and made a film with her there: *The Big Boodle*. Later, she become the girlfriend of Marlon Brando and appeared with him in a film. She obviously had talent.

RICHARD GREENE'S
SHERWOOD FOREST VISITOR

British actor Richard Greene starred in *The Adventures of Robin Hood*, the number-one TV series around the world between 1955 and 1959. In the mid-1950s, when I was running my publicity office in London, we were good friends and, although I never did represent him, I saw him frequently for a rather unusual reason.

Robin Hood was filmed at the Walton-on-Thames Studios, only a few hundred yards away from my home at 75 Hersham Road in Walton. My wife, our two very young children, and I lived in one of six apartments made from an old mansion, the grounds of which had about ten acres overlooking Walton village green.

This location was an asset from my point of view, because of its proximity—a one-minute walk–to the Walton train station, which got me to London every day in less than twenty minutes. But from Richard Greene's point of view, 75 Hersham Road had another great asset: a huge oak tree, surrounded by a mini forest, in front of the house. It was this oak tree that the producers of *Robin Hood* chose to be the meeting place of Robin and his Merry Men. These included Paul Eddington, who played Will Scarlett, and later became much more famous in two TV series still being shown in Canada today: *Yes Minister* and *Yes, Prime Minister*.

Greene, who I had met through my friendship with Richard Burton, often dropped in with Paul Eddington for a cup of tea during shooting.

Paul liked the old mansion so much, he later leased the apartment next to ours and lived there as a good neighbour until we left England. He remained there until the beautiful building was demolished some twenty years later.

I saw a lot of Richard Greene, Paul Eddington, and Donald Pleasance (who played Prince John) because they were all appearing in plays in London at the time, and weekend overtime shooting for *Robin Hood* was a common thing. Regularly on Sundays, when I was home, the unit descended on 75 Hersham Road to film yet one more oak tree session with Robin Hood.

In those days the unions were not as strict as they are now, and most of Robin Hood's Merry Men were my friends and neighbours from the other apartments or nearby houses, who enjoyed receiving the one-day pay of ten pounds as extras. (Yes, I earned a few tenners myself.) Towards the end of the *Robin Hood* era, Errol Flynn started filming his own TV series at the nearby Bray Film Studios.

★

When Errol Flynn's son, Sean, came over from the United States to visit him, Errol and Patrice drove him over to 75 Hersham Road one Sunday morning for lunch. It was one of the days the *Robin Hood* unit also paid a visit. The call came out for extras for the day's shooting and Patrice suggested, as a joke, that she, Errol, and Sean should volunteer.

The man in charge of the costume truck didn't recognize them and they were fitted out appropriately. Flynn was not as young and handsome as he had once been, and not a soul on the set recognized him— although Alexander Gauge, who played Friar Tuck, did say to Errol, "You could get a good stand-in job at Bray Studios for Errol Flynn. At times, you look just like him. I'll give you the casting director's phone number if you are interested."

Flynn managed to get in just about every scene; deliberately pulling grotesque faces when he knew the camera was directly on him. At the end of shooting, Flynn went over to Richard Greene, whom he had never met, pulled his hat down over his face to disguise himself, and asked Greene to sign his ten-pound note.

"I'll probably never appear in another TV show," said Flynn. "I want to keep this as a souvenir." Greene signed, wished him luck, and asked if he was just a local man or an actor. I'll never forget Flynn's response. "Actor? Me?" he said. "Nobody has ever accused me of being that!" Flynn still had the ten-pound autographed note in his wallet when he died in Vancouver several years later.

The following Tuesday, my office phone rang. It was Richard Greene. "You pulled one on me," he said. "You should see the film from Sunday. There's that joker Flynn leering over my shoulder in half a dozen scenes. We're going to leave the scenes in because they are so funny. But I can't let him get away with it. How do I repay him?"

Over the next two days, Richard Greene and I cooked up a plot that those fortunate enough to own the videos of the *Errol Flynn Theatre* TV series can still laugh at today.

That particular week, Flynn was playing the role of an old farmer in a script I had written. In one scene, Flynn is found sitting outside an old pub with a bottle of beer in his hand. Suddenly Robin Hood, fully costumed from his own series, appears on the set riding a bicycle we had borrowed from a local store. He stops by Flynn (we had alerted the director to the gag and told the cameraman to keep shooting) and says, "Could you direct me to Sherwood Forest, old chap?" Flynn, who must have been shocked, was never at a loss for words: "Sherwood Forest? Yes, it's right down there at 75 Hersham Road."

As Robin Hood rode away, the director yelled, "Cut," and everyone broke up in gales of laughter.

We got a lot of publicity in the press for both series when we told the story, and both scenes were left in the shows. Ratings were the highest ever...except in the United States. There, the two shows appeared on different networks and the totally uncooperative companies didn't see our joke as the least bit humorous. Both shows cut out what was surely one of the funniest jokes of the season.

28

A GLASS OF MILK SAVED
ERROL FLYNN'S CAREER

Errol Flynn was coming to the end of his illustrious career by this time—the 1950s—when he arrived in England to start filming his TV series. But his name still had a magical effect, and news of his arrival brought constant requests to my publicity office for interviews. I had no difficulty getting stories printed in British papers, and I wrote and placed dozens more through the Associated Press in the North American market, where the show was to be televised by NBC.

Bray Studio, where the series was filmed, was a former small-feature film studio that had been converted to TV production. It was about fifty kilometres west of London. The production company provided Flynn with a car and driver each morning for the ten-minute drive from the Bray hotel where he, his wife Patrice, and his son Sean were staying.

Errol was happy at first. The first two scripts, which he had seen before leaving his home in Rome for England, were both well-written. But his enthusiasm waned when he received scripts three and four. My home phone rang at ten at night on the Wednesday of the week before filming was scheduled for script three.

"Hey Sport," said Flynn. "I need you, fast!"

I drove from my home in Walton-on-Thames to Bray—normally a thirty-minute journey—in less than fifteen minutes. From the sound of Errol's voice, something was seriously wrong.

"Read this," he said. While I read script three, he downed at least three glasses of whisky. When I had finished reading, I told him I agreed. "The script is terrible. I could do better myself."

"Think so? Then take it home and bring your version to the studio before noon tomorrow," said Flynn. "Work all night if you have to but I want something to show our producer that is better than the staff writer's feeble effort."

Until that moment, I had never written a television script, but I drove home and started work. By five in the morning I had my script ready. I slept for three hours, then drove to the studio in Bray.

"Well," said Flynn, "did you do it?"

"Yes," I replied. "Here, read it for yourself. You may think this is worse than their effort. Remember, it's the first I've ever written."

He took it and a smile began to creep over his face.

"I love it," he said. "I'll take this over to the producer and tell him this is the script we will be using next week, or I walk off the set for good."

The producer read the script and he, too, smiled. "We'll use it," he said to Flynn. "Get Charlie to read the next two scripts and rewrite those. If they're good, we'll use them too."

I wrote four more scripts for *The Errol Flynn Theatre*: two rewrites of terrible official scripts and two originals. All were accepted and all were filmed. Suddenly I had become a television scriptwriter. The series didn't do well in the United States, and after ten weeks, NBC said they were taking it off the air. Production was halted at Bray and my foray into scriptwriting ended immediately.

Flynn wasn't too concerned. He had heard that producer Darryl Zanuck was about to produce, in Mexico, Spain, and France, *The Sun Also Rises*, an adaptation of the Ernest Hemingway book of the same name.

"I want the role of Mike Campbell in that film," he said. "It's made for me. In fact, it *is* me."

I called on another of my wartime contacts in Hollywood for help. Jack Warner, who admired Flynn, was still in command at Warner Brothers in the film capital, and he promised to sound out Darryl

Zanuck. Within an hour, he called me back with bad news.

"Zanuck agrees that Campbell is the perfect role for Flynn, but he's been getting reports from London that Flynn is drinking heavily again. Unless you can prove that he isn't, Zanuck won't consider him."

I devised a simple plan to convince Zanuck. Every night, Flynn and I went to the bar at the Dorchester Hotel in London, and other regular patrons were surprised to see him with nothing but a bottle of milk on his table, from which he constantly refilled his glass. No liquor was in sight. I called my good friend Bob Dear, chief photographer at the Associated Press, and told him there was a great picture to be shot at the Dorchester bar every night. Bob took the hint and grabbed a shot of Flynn drinking milk. The Associated Press sent it out to America. Hundreds of papers, including the *Los Angeles Times*, used it on their front pages.

Jack Warner made sure Darryl Zanuck saw it.

"I've news from London that Flynn is on the wagon," he told Zanuck. "Better sign him now for that role in *The Sun Also Rises* before he gets snapped up by someone else."

Zanuck contacted Henry King, who was scheduled to direct the film. King was in London staying at the Dorchester Hotel; after viewing Flynn drinking milk for five straight nights, he called Zanuck and told him Flynn appeared to have reformed. Within days, Flynn was asked to sign a contract for the role he so badly wanted.

Although Tyrone Power and Ava Gardner were the official stars of the film, it was Errol Flynn who walked away with all the best reviews. Zanuck was so delighted he immediately signed Flynn to a role in another major film and Errol was back on top in Hollywood.

In London the milk story had spread, and we actually had to turn down a request by the British Milk Marketing Board to use Flynn as their spokesman for a "drink more milk" campaign. What none of them knew was that the "milk" Flynn was drinking was supplied by me to the Dorchester Hotel's head bartender each evening, to be put in a cooler until Flynn arrived. The "milk" was nothing more than pure vodka, made—with the help of a local pharmacist—to look like milk. We kept a real bottle of milk in the Dorchester bar refrigerator, in case anyone asked to check out Flynn's new beverage of choice. As far as I know, our plan was never challenged and the real milk was eventually put down the drain.

I never did tell Bob Dear at AP I had pulled a fast one on him with the story. So, much as I regretted hearing of Bob's demise some years ago, I am rather glad he is not around now to get his revenge.

WHEN THE DUKE OF BEDFORD GOT LOST ON THE JUNGFRAU

When the thirteenth Duke of Bedford—fifty-seventh in line for the British throne—died a few years ago at the age of eighty-five, show business lost one of its greatest personalities. He attended official functions with all the dignity of the Royal Family, but in his brain at all times was a mischievous, slightly wicked disposition that was definitely not royal, and he created many delightful moments with his humour.

Many years ago when I was running my publicity company in London, he walked into my office.

"I need your help," he said. "I'm the Duke of Bedford, but I prefer to use my family name. Introduce me to your staff as Ian Russell and tell everyone to call me Ian."

A few years earlier, he had inherited the family's magnificent ancestral castle, Woburn Abbey, near Bedford, England. With that inheritance came death duties totalling more than £2 million, which he and his family did not have. To raise the money, he opened the castle to the public, charging ten shillings for a guided tour of the wonderful buildings. More often than not, the guide was the duke himself. But for some reason, Woburn Abbey had never really caught the imagination of the public.

"I made a lot of money from admissions the first year, selling ice cream, pop, and sandwiches, and I posed for Polaroid pictures with guests for a pound, signing the photos for another ten shillings," he said. "But it isn't enough. I want to be able to keep all the abbey treasures and one day hand them down to my son. I want you to devise some publicity ideas that will bring in ten times the visitors I had this year. Will you do it?"

I'd heard many good things about the duke, so I didn't hesitate. I was working at the time on a British/American TV series, *Dick and the Duchess*, and the day after we spoke I took him to the studio to have pictures taken with Patrick O'Neal, the US star. The photos were printed in many papers in the United States and England, and as summer was just starting, the American visitors to Woburn began to increase in number. But neither Ian nor I was satisfied. We had to do something truly dramatic to put him and his Woburn Abbey in the headlines and once more in the black.

Paramount had asked me to publicize a new film—*High Hell*—then in production, starring John Derek and Elaine Stewart. Both were big celebrities at that time. The actors and production crew were scheduled to fly from London to Switzerland in two days for a week's location shooting, and I was to go with them.

"How would you like a week in Switzerland?" I asked Ian. "I promise I'll find some way to put the trip, and you, on the front pages."

"Sounds good," he said. "But I can't act, so forget any ideas of that happening."

Two days into the location shooting, the film unit was hit by bad weather. Everyone was sitting around playing poker in the lounge of a beautiful hotel on top of the thirteen thousand-foot Jungfrau mountain (where we were filming), when Elaine Stewart, looking out of the window, winced a little. "Thank heaven I'm not going out in that blizzard," she said.

Suddenly I had my story! "But you are going out, Elaine—you and the Duke of Bedford. We'll add in Harry Claff, our makeup man, for good measure. Let's have a talk."

An hour later we had our front-page story all set. Ian, Elaine, Harry, and the donkey, which we were using in the film, were to be announced as "lost" in the blizzard on top of the Jungfrau.

I called Bob Dear at the Associated Press in London to give him the scoop and added that a local guide working for the film company, Hans Egger, and Billy Boyle, the film's producer, were out looking for them. The AP put out the story and called constantly to ask for updates. It made headlines around the world. Both Elaine and Ian were well-known and Harry Claff became an overnight celebrity. (Harry was later flown to New York to appear on TV interview shows, where he turned out to be the best actor on the unit. He could have made a fortune in Hollywood as a character actor from the way he described the rescue that never really happened.)

Finally, we decided it was time to rescue the missing group. Much to her dismay, Elaine had her glorious hair tousled and covered in snow; Ian and Harry suffered the same fate. The poor donkey was the only one unconcerned. Apparently he had experienced worse storms in the past. The AP had urged that our stills cameraman be ready to take pictures when and if the group was rescued. So we set it all up and announced to the AP that they had been found and were being brought back to the hotel. Bob Dear asked that the undeveloped film be put on the mountain railway immediately, where he would arrange for it to be collected in Grindelwald. Somehow they got it to London the same day and distributed our masterpiece worldwide.

We had a conference before the calls started, and I wrote a script that basically told the same story from each participant's different point of view. Newspapers from around the world called to speak to Ian, Elaine, Harry, and Hans. Even Billy Boyle spoke to them. Every line to the hotel was blocked for hours. For three days, we made front-page news with the rescue picture and quotes from the "lost" and their rescuers, Hans and Billy.

The next day, Ian went back to London. He told me by phone that he was met at the airport by more than fifty newspapers reporters and photographers, and camera crews from all the TV stations. "Maybe I should take up acting," he said. "I convinced the press I nearly lost my life. I also convinced them to tell their readers that if they want to meet me I will be at Woburn Abbey all summer to show them my beautiful home."

He actually beat me with his imaginative mind. When I visited him at Woburn, he invited me to see something special. There, in a beautiful grassy area, was a donkey. It was labelled with a sign that read: *The donkey that saved the Duke of Bedford's life.*

"Ian," I said, "how on earth did you get the donkey over here from Switzerland?"

"I didn't," he said.

"Then where did you get this animal?"

"Bought it from a local farmer. I didn't think it was too unreasonable, since the main story we all benefitted from was just as phony."

Business that summer was so great he had to hire security guards to keep the crowds in order.

★

Paramount was happy, Ian was delighted, and Elaine basked in her new publicity and—even in those more sedate days—didn't deny that she and Ian might be a twosome. (That resulted in another story that only Ian's wife was unhappy about.)

I was well paid, and received clippings from more than two hundred newspapers and magazines from around the world. The official donkey was taken down the mountain to Grindelwald, where it led a luxurious life being fed and photographed by adoring tourists who had read our story (which claimed that had the donkey not forced the "missing group" to stop in the raging storm, they would have gone over the edge of a cliff in the blizzard). The only unhappy person was John Derek. He still won't talk to me, nor will his beautiful wife of that time, Ursula Andress, who was in Switzerland with him, because I did not include them in the story.

Because of the success of the publicity, Ian was invited back to the set of the TV series *Dick and the Duchess*. This time he was greeted not by the stars but by our rather glamorous French-born producer, Nicole Milinaire. She had not been around on his first visit, but this day she certainly was. By the end of Ian's visit, Nicole had taken over as his guide. At the wrap-up of shooting, when I suggested to Ian that it was time to go home, he said, "Don't worry about me, I'm going to dinner with Nicole. She'll see me home safely."

I saw him often after that, but had left England and was in my new home in Toronto, Canada, a few years later when I bumped into him quite accidentally at the Toronto Airport. I was waiting for a friend from Vancouver when I heard a familiar voice yelling at me from the British Overseas Airways counter.

Ian had arrived in Canada to help promote the book he had written about beautiful Woburn Abbey. Minutes later, after I discovered my expected friend from the west had missed his flight, Ian and I headed into Toronto to the Royal York Hotel, where he was to stay.

"Just the man I need," he said in the car. "Will you help me promote my book and Woburn Abbey in the three days I am here in Canada?"

Of course I said yes, and prepared for a lot of fun, but it was the shock I received while we were sitting in his suite at the hotel later that evening that made the visit most memorable.

The phone in the suite rang. "Do me a favour: as my official publicist, you now take all my phone calls. It will probably be someone wanting an interview."

But it wasn't. The call came from the *Daily Mail* in London. The caller said he wished to speak to the duke.

"Is there a special reason?" I asked.

"Certainly is. We have just been told the Duchess of Bedford has filed for divorce and we want the duke's side of the story."

I asked him to hold, and told Ian what the call was about.

"Well, you deal with him," said Ian. "After all, you are entirely responsible."

"Me, responsible?" I asked. "How can I be responsible for something like this?"

"You introduced me to the woman I am going to marry once Lydia [the duchess] gets out of Woburn."

I hadn't a clue who he was talking about.

"Who did I introduce you to?" I asked.

"Nicole Milinaire," he responded. "I never did get home that night after visiting the TV studio, and things have gone downhill at Woburn ever since. And by the way, you may also be responsible for my son Robin getting married next year. Remember that beautiful young American girl, Henrietta, you brought over to Woburn a couple of years ago? Robin is going to marry her. He told me so last week." (Henrietta Tiarks was the daughter of a multi-millionaire financier from New York. She had been put in my charge by her parents when she visited England alone on vacation.)

So dare I say that the future Dukes of Bedford definitely have me to label responsible for their existence? I like to think so. I hardly knew Robin, but Ian was a wonderful, kind man, and Henrietta was a delightful young lady who made a week of my life in London most pleasant.

After Ian left Woburn in 1973, just prior to his death, Robin and Henrietta moved in and soon after became the fourteenth Duke and Duchess of Bedford. Shockingly, Robin had a heart attack and died unexpectedly in 2003, and the fifteenth Duke and Dutchess—Robin and Henrietta's son, Andrew, and his wife, Louise—inherited the title, hopefully to live there for many years.

The former Henrietta Tiarks is still living on the estate and plays a major role each summer ensuring that it remains one of the most popular tourist attractions in England. Hello, Henrietta! Do you still remember me? I certainly haven't forgotten you.

THE SECRET CHARLIE CHAPLIN
KEPT FOR FIFTY YEARS

.

I had kept in touch with Charlie Chaplin by mail for more than a decade after our memorable meeting in Hollywood during the Second World War; and when I wrote him in 1949 at his new home in Vevey, Switzerland, to say how disgusted I was that the United States government had refused to allow him back into America, I received a phone call thanking me.

"You are one of the few supporting me," he said. "I will not forget that."

Claiming Chaplin owed millions in unpaid taxes, the United States cancelled his return entry visa when he visited Europe on vacation. It took years for Chaplin to prove that he did not owe a cent before he was finally invited back to receive a lifetime Oscar for his work in the film industry.

Four years later, he proved that he indeed had not forgotten. Once again, my home phone rang. "Charlie Chaplin here," said the easily recognizable voice. "I am coming to London in a few weeks to make a new film. I hear from friends that your publicity office is a great success and I want your services to help re-establish me in the eyes of the Americans."

Working with Charlie Chaplin was a dream everyone in the industry hoped would one day come true, and within days I was called to the office of a London lawyer to be officially announced as not only

Chaplin's publicist on his proposed film, A King In New York, but also his personal assistant. I won't tell you how much I was paid, for in today's world of immense salaries it would sound like a pittance. Let me just say that his offer was enough to pay my entire office of three people, including myself, for the entire year.

The five weeks I worked with him were some of the most fascinating and enjoyable of my life. I met him at London's Heathrow Airport and drove him to the Savoy Hotel. I had already read the script and had to admit to Chaplin that I was a little wary of some of the content. I remember saying to him, "Charlie, you are the world's greatest comedian and some of the script is not very funny. Why are you doing this?"

"Don't forget, they have exiled me from my home in California," he said. "I think it is time I told the truth in a film."

There was no arguing with Chaplin. And besides, to argue with such a giant—perhaps one of the most renowned actors and directors of all time—was obviously not a very intelligent thing to do. I arranged two press conferences to announce the film. These brought worldwide publicity. For the first time in years, Charlie Chaplin's face was on the front pages of newspapers around the world—including, to Chaplin's delight, the United States.

Once shooting started, no more interviews were allowed. I saw how Chaplin had made himself such a giant in the film industry. Nothing was to interrupt the filming. Studio gates were locked; inside, it was rather like being in a prison. But slowly, to me at least, it became obvious that A King in New York was not up to the usual Charlie Chaplin standards. Something was missing. It was the comedic touch that I had dared to mention en route from the airport to the hotel some weeks earlier. There was a bitterness in the film that, in my opinion, had no place in the comedic world that had made Chaplin so great.

When the film was ready for its opening night, it took almost eight months for Chaplin to find a small theatre on Oxford Street willing to show it. The big London theatres, all of which depended on getting American films to fill their seats, refused to show the film. I spoke to a couple theatre owners, and they admitted that pressure from the

United States had forced them to refuse to open their doors to *A King in New York*.

Only one of the British actors in the cast, Sidney James, attended the opening night. Sidney said he didn't care if Chaplin was black-listed forever in the US, and that it had been an honour to work with him and he intended to be at the premiere. One of the other main actors admitted to me that the US distributors told her none of her future films would ever be shown in the United States if she attended the premiere. "What could I do?" she said. "My entire career depends on exposure in the US."

But the theatre was full.

Every penny taken at the box office that night went to charity, and there were some big names in the audience—but only Sidney James from the film industry. As the audience left, Charlie shook hands with every one of the seven hundred attendees. When the last patron had gone, Chaplin and I stood alone in the theatre lobby with the owner.

It was a beautiful night and Chaplin suggested we walk back to the Savoy Hotel. It was obvious to him that the audience had been restless and that *A King in New York* was not going to be one of his most memorable productions. He was silent at first as we walked along Oxford Street. Then suddenly, he turned and hailed a taxi that was cruising by.

He gave a huge smile. "Charlie," he said, "I want to show you something nobody but me has ever seen before." He instructed the driver: "Take us to Collins Music Hall in Islington." Again he fell silent. But as we neared the end of our twenty-minute drive to the oldest music hall still standing in England, he began to smile again. "Tonight's disaster is over," he said. "Now I'm going to show you what I thought of my future fifty years ago."

The cab dropped us at the entrance to Collins. As we walked into the lobby, the performers appearing there in a musical revue were well into their second performance of the evening. The entrance lobby was completely empty. Nobody saw us as Chaplin grabbed my arm and pulled me into the men's washroom right by the long-closed box office.

We entered. Not a soul was there.

"Good, it's empty," he said.

He walked across the room to an iron door in the corner. Yanking it open, he led me into a long passageway dimly lit by three very dusty light bulbs. The passageway led from the washroom right underneath the auditorium to the edge of the stage and to another closed iron door. We could clearly hear the theatre orchestra and the tapping of the dancers' feet on the stage that was almost above us. Chaplin looked intently at the brick wall. He pulled a pen out of his pocket and used it to dislodge a loose brick. As it fell to the ground, he reached into the cavity and brought out a small, metal tobacco box.

He pushed the box into my hand.

"Open it," he said.

Inside, I found a folded piece of yellowed paper. On it were these words: *I, Charles Spencer Chaplin, appeared at Collins Music Hall on this day, January 17, 1907. Today I am a nobody. One day I will be the world's most important comedian.* It was signed, *Charles Spencer Chaplin.*

"See, I knew even then," said Chaplin. He went silent a moment. "Until tonight, when I lost my touch with *A King in New York.*"

He wiped away the tear that ran down his cheek.

"May I keep this?" I asked.

"No," said Chaplin. "It must remain here until I am dead. Then I would like you to come back here and retrieve it and show it to the world." He returned the note to the box and put the box back into the wall, carefully replacing the brick he had removed earlier.

We left the theatre and grabbed another taxi back to the Savoy. He never again mentioned the box in the wall of Collins Music Hall. Sadly, *A King In New York* did not receive favourable reviews in the British press, and so far as I know was never mentioned or shown in the United States.

I was living in New Brunswick when Chaplin died in 1977. I wrote to Oona, his wife, in Vevey, but never did receive a reply. Four years later, when I returned to England to attend a RAF reunion in London, I decided to visit Collins Music Hall once more to see if I could re-cover Charlie Chaplin's remarkable prediction. The door from the men's washroom to the passageway was locked. The theatre manager was sympathetic when I explained my mission but said it would be dangerous to open the door, as part of the passageway had collapsed several years earlier. "It is impossible to get down there now," he said.

Collins Music Hall is no longer there. It was razed to the ground following a fire some years later. To the best of my knowledge, Chaplin's historic prediction is somewhere in the rubble that once was the great Collins Music Hall. Sadly, I fear it will never be retrieved.

SMUGGLING MARILYN
INTO LONDON

I had bumped into Laurence Olivier a few times at opening nights and other functions following the incident with Richard Burton at the opening of his play *Much Ado About Everything*, back in 1945. He had always been polite, never once referring to the moment Jimmy Edwards and I nearly destroyed the opening night's performance. But Olivier had never offered my publicity office work on any of his films, and so I presumed he still remembered the episode and that I would never have the chance to call him a client.

In 1957 I read in the London newspapers that Marilyn Monroe had agreed to co-star with Olivier in a new film to be produced by Olivier's British company, Laurence Olivier Productions (LOP) Ltd. The story said the film would be shot at Pinewood Studios in North London. I presumed Olivier's production company had its own publicist, and in view of Olivier's lack of interest in my growing successes, I gave no more thought to the story or Monroe's visit. So it was a shock when I picked up my office phone to hear the unmistakable voice of Laurence Olivier greeting me.

"Charles," he said, "I hope you have time to accept a little job I would like to offer you. I want you to look after the publicity on my new film, *The Prince and the Showgirl*, in which I will star with Marilyn Monroe. It will be rather an unusual job for a publicist, because Monroe's Los Angeles agent has insisted a clause be put in her contract that at no time during our five-week production schedule will she be made to give interviews to or be photographed by the news media. And that apparently means all media.

"This will probably be the first client you have ever had who doesn't want publicity. Apparently she just wants to be left alone. It may turn out to be a tough job, but I promise you—money will be no object. First I need your help to get Marilyn through Heathrow Airport tomorrow morning without going through customs or meeting the press.

"Somehow we have to get her to the house I have rented for her at Englefield Green in Surrey without them knowing where we are taking her. I am told you are the only publicist in London who can find a way to do what she asks. Will you accept the work?"

Olivier told me how much I would be paid—plus all expenses incurred with no limits to what I could spend—so I had no hesitation in accepting. I was to have five hundred pounds in my wallet at all times, which Olivier would provide, so that if Marilyn asked for anything to be purchased, I would be able, without question, to pay for it. Remember, this was before credit cards.

Meeting Marilyn Monroe was a delightful prospect. She was a major personality in the world of show business. But I had only twenty-four hours to figure out a way to beat the news media waiting at Heathrow, who had certainly already been alerted by Trans-World Airlines that she was to be aboard one of their planes from New York.

I called Olivier back three hours later. "Is there is a large lawn at the house you have rented?"

"Very large," said Olivier, "why?"

"I have convinced British customs officials to check through Monroe's hand baggage before she leaves the plane. I will have somebody at customs to see her checked baggage through immigration and have everything delivered to my office in London. There, it will be loaded aboard my car and delivered to her in Englefield Green with only she, you, and I knowing where she will be staying. Having cleared customs on board, Monroe will leave the plane and step into a waiting limousine that will take her to a helicopter on the other side of the airfield. The helicopter, piloted by a good friend who will keep his mouth shut, will fly her to the house you have rented—just a ten-minute flight—where you and I will be waiting to greet her.

"Not a single news reporter will have seen her, and once she is safely in the house we can take the rest of her stay from there."

Olivier was delighted. "Incredible," he said. "You have just earned an extra five hundred pounds. Now, how do we get her to the studio each day without anyone knowing where she is staying?"

"I will drive my own car from Walton-on-Thames to Englefield Green—just fifteen minutes—pick her up and drive her to the studio every morning," I said. "The whole trip should take less than an hour. What time will you want her there?"

"She must be at Pinewood no later than nine o'clock. That will give her an hour in makeup with a hairstylist, and into costume so she can shoot her first scene around ten."

The plan worked like a dream. The news media at London Airport only discovered that we had whisked her away by helicopter after it was already in the air. Nobody but me, Olivier, the helicopter pilot, and the housekeeper Olivier had hired, knew where Marilyn was staying.

★

Marilyn Monroe turned out to be a delight. She was completely down-to-earth. Her only request was that I buy a not-too-easy jigsaw puzzle, because she loved them. I spent hours working with her on the most complicated ones I could find. Because of Marilyn, I have a love of jigsaws that continues to this day.

We had a few days to spare before shooting started, and on each of those days I drove Marilyn to Olivier's North London home so they could go through the script at their leisure. Other members of the cast met her there for the first time and, like me, found her delightful and totally co-operative. When I asked her why she wanted to elude the press, she said, "You can't imagine what it is like in Hollywood. Photographers follow me everywhere; they sit outside my bedroom window. A little time alone will be like landing in paradise."

I was given a key to the Englefield Green house, since the house-keeper went home every night at six and didn't return the next day until nine in the morning, and we had to be on our way to the studio no later than eight. Marilyn was left alone in the house overnight until I arrived the next morning. Olivier offered to supply security guards, but Marilyn said no. "It's just so wonderful being alone," she said. "I've dreamed about being alone in a big house all my life, and now it has come true. I'll be quite safe."

Everything went perfectly—until the morning of the first day of shooting at Pinewood. That morning gave me the surprise of my life—and as Marilyn told me a number of times later when I was living in Hollywood, the biggest shock of her entire life. This was the day I discovered that Marilyn always told the truth. It was a delightful discovery that could have ended my career as a publicist, but instead made me a friend for life.

A MEMORABLE MORNING
WITH MARILYN

I became more and more enthused about working with Marilyn Monroe in the days that followed her arrival at the beautiful home Laurence Olivier had rented for her in Englefield Green. The house was a forty-minute car ride from Pinewood Studios in North London, where she was to film *The Prince and the Showgirl* with Olivier.

She unfailingly read and re-read her lines at home each evening after rehearsing them during the day at Olivier's mansion near the studio. I spent many pleasant hours going over the script line by line with her. It is such a vivid memory that I still recall most of the dialogue to this day.

One evening, on the way home from Olivier's, we passed a bicycle shop. "Stop the car, Charlie, please," she said. She jumped out and went directly to a tandem bicycle. "I can ride a bicycle, but have always wanted one of these two-seaters," she said. "Buy it, please—then we can ride around the beautiful English countryside at weekends."

Fortunately I had the five hundred pounds in my wallet. The bicycle dealer strapped our purchase to the top of my car. "The lady does look like Marilyn Monroe," he said. "Could she perhaps be Miss Monroe's stand-in?"

"Yes," said Marilyn. "I am. Do I really look like her?"

"Spitting image," he said.

As we drove away, she said, "Spitting, I hate spitting. That's why my marriage to Joe Di Maggio broke up. He was nice, but he was always spitting. Baseball players do."

I had to explain that "spitting image" means "almost identical."

"I like that," she said. "Perhaps I made a mistake divorcing Joe."

We spent many weekends riding around the countryside. She covered her blond hair with a huge scarf and wore no makeup at all. If people thought she looked like Marilyn Monroe, they probably said to each other: "It can't be…Marilyn Monroe would never be riding on a tandem bicycle around Surrey."

Marilyn was clever. When she got tired of pedalling, she just rested her feet on the front pedals and let them go around from the momentum of my hard pedalling in the rear. She would smile around at me. "Getting tired are you, Charlie? See, I'm not tired at all." But riding around on the seat behind Marilyn was certainly not hard to take; I hoped she knew where we were going, because my eyes were not looking at the countryside.

★

On the first day of shooting at Pinewood, I arrived at the Englefield Green house at about a quarter to eight in the morning. I expected to find Marilyn ready for an early start. She had been making her own breakfasts—scrambled eggs and toast with orange juice—since she had arrived, and enjoyed the freedom of being able to perform that simple chore. But that morning she was nowhere to be seen.

I shouted her name a few times before looking in the bedroom in which she slept. There she was, fast asleep in bed. I went over to the bed and shook her. She opened one eye and half-smiled. "I stayed up late with the jigsaw," she said. "I need at least another hour's sleep."

I warned her it wouldn't look good if she arrived at Pinewood late on the first day of shooting.

"Why?" she said. "Larry won't mind—I'm the star, aren't I?"

I told her I was going to put water in the bathtub and wanted her out of bed in two minutes. When the tub was full, and at what I considered a reasonable temperature, I went back into the bedroom. She was fast asleep again.

I shook her until she was wide awake. "Marilyn," I said, "don't let Larry Olivier down! Please, get up right now."

She smiled. "And what if I don't? What will you do about it?"

I smiled back. "Marilyn," I said, "I'm going to give you thirty seconds and then I'm going to pull you out of bed, carry you to the bathroom, and drop you in the bathtub."

Her eyes opened wide. "You daren't," she said. "Nobody would dare do that to me."

"Oh yes, I dare," I said.

She made no move, so after a minute or two I yanked back the bedclothes ,and there was Monroe, sleeping as she had often said, wearing nothing but Chanel N°5.

I picked her up, and she put her arms around my neck and gave me a big kiss. "You daren't drop me in the tub," she said.

I carried her into the bathroom and unceremoniously dumped her into the water.

She screamed and then lazily smiled. "I like you, Charlie," she said. "You do keep your promises, don't you?"

By then I figured I really ought to get out of the bathroom. But I backed out slowly...I wasn't in any hurry to lose the view.

In ten minutes, she was ready to get in the car. I made her a fried-egg sandwich, which she ate on the way to the studio. We arrived at the gates of Pinewood Studios at exactly 9 A.M. She was in hairdressing at 9:10 and was ready to shoot the first scene at 10 A.M.

Olivier, who obviously had been warned that Marilyn wasn't an early riser, asked if I'd had any problems.

"Problems? Oh dear, no," I said. "Absolutely no problems. In fact, I would like to say just the opposite!"

Sadly, I must tell you that every other morning during the five-week shooting schedule, Marilyn was waiting at the door when I arrived to pick her up.

I received letters from her regularly after she returned to the United States. You will be astonished to know that in almost every letter, she asked me for advice about something or other, often very personal things. Why I was chosen for this honour I shall never know.

We met again often when I was living in California, and there was one occasion, when she dropped in to my apartment unexpectedly, when I introduced her to an equally unexpected visitor I had never thought would be my guest. I have often feared it was that introduction that led to her untimely death only a few years later.

SPARKY TAUGHT ME
THE SECRETS OF BASEBALL

It isn't until you pick up the paper to see the name of a friend who is no longer in the land of the living that you begin to realize maybe your own days on earth could be numbered too. No matter how well you feel, you know that the person whose name you have just seen in the obits column is no older than you— and often, sadly, much younger.

In the past few years, I have lost many friends. Some are those I have worked with, like Elizabeth Taylor, singer Al Martino, comedian Benny Hill, director Ken Annakin, the delightful Connie Hines (Carol Post in *Mr. Ed*), and of course, the man who really put my career as a writer into top gear: Paul Henning, the creator of *The Beverly Hillbillies*. But a letter from a friend in Detroit who is a great baseball fan reminded me of someone not in show business who played an important part in my life more than fifty years ago. This friend asked if I had ever met the wonderful baseball manager Sparky Anderson, who became a legend in his own time during his tenure with the Detroit Tigers. I was happy to tell him the story I am about to tell you now.

When I first came over to Canada in 1958, Jack Kent Cooke at Radio CKEY in Toronto hired me as his publicity director. Our sports director, Joe Crysdale, invited me to accompany him to the Toronto Maple Leafs—the forerunner of today's Major League Blue Jays—baseball stadium, which Cooke also owned, where Joe broadcast nightly games for the International League. I knew nothing about baseball. As you're already aware, I had never, back in 1943, heard of Babe Ruth: my games were cricket and soccer. But I thought I should learn about this new game that everyone seemed to love.

On my first night at the stadium, Jack Cooke came over to me. "Glad to see you like baseball," he said. "One day I shall own a major league franchise, and I will need you as my publicist." To my regret now, when that did happen in 1967, and he owned the Los Angeles Kings, I actually turned down his offer. I had to admit to Jack that I didn't know a bunt from a four-bagger or a spitter from a curveball. So he decided to introduce me to the man I am writing about today: Sparky Anderson.

Yes, believe it or not, Sparky Anderson was once the opening bat for the Toronto Maple Leafs. He had played one season in the majors for the Philadelphia Phillies, but only batted .218, and so was sent to Toronto. That was in 1959. I must comment here that the many stories that have been told about how Sparky (whose real name was George Lee) got his name are mostly phony. He was Sparky back in 1959 when he played in Toronto, regardless of what any official records tell you. He once told me that a radio announcer called him that when he was only twenty-one and playing for the Fort Worth Cats in the Texas League.

Sparky was rather appalled that I didn't know anything about baseball, and decided, with Jack Cooke's approval, to remove me from the press box and sit me down on the team bench next to him throughout the game. Thanks to Sparky Anderson I very quickly became not only enthused with baseball, but knowledgeable too.

Sparky was an encyclopedia of information. He told me when it was time for a hit and run, when a player should bunt, when to watch the runner on second who was about to steal third, and when the pitcher was making mistakes. I came to the conclusion that Sparky Anderson, who really wasn't a great baseball player, should be a manager. I remember one evening telling Jack Cooke that I was grateful I had been allowed to sit on the bench, but that although Sparky could tell me everything about the game, he often made the same mistakes at bat, in the field, and at second base that he chastised others for making.

"I think Sparky is one day going to be a wonderful manager," I told Jack.

"Think I don't know that?" he responded. "I've been watching him for a long time. He has more knowledge of this game than anyone I have ever known."

For those of you who don't know, Jack Cooke did not forget the talents of Sparky Anderson. Jack kept tabs on him, and it was he who gave Sparky his first managerial job as the boss of the Toronto Maple Leafs in 1964. It was there that major league owners first noticed his managerial skills, and it was then that his career as a manager first began.

★

Sparky and I became great friends. He used to come to my publicity office at CKEY, put his feet on the desk, and say: "Your turn now! Explain to me about this rock 'n' roll music that the young people seem to like." When young stars like Paul Anka, Johnny Cash, Johnny Mathis, the Platters, or Conway Twitty were scheduled to visit the studio, Sparky wanted to know in advance so he could meet them. In turn he introduced me to a lot of people, including a baseball player named Rocky Nelson. (Okay, so today you don't even remember this fine baseballer. But I do, and I thank my lucky stars I can say now I once was his friend.)

Rocky, a wonderful hitter, went from the Toronto Maple Leafs to the White Sox, then the Pirates—during which time he was in the 1960 World Series—Dodgers, Indians, and Cardinals. I kept in touch, and from time to time he would call to say hello.

I often saw Sparky in Thousand Oaks, near Los Angeles, where he had made his home—even when he was at the height of his success in Detroit—and we would watch a game at the Los Angeles Angels baseball stadium in Anaheim, where Gene Autry has given me a permanent pass. His home was just two doors away from my old friend from the *Beverly Hillbillies*, Buddy Ebsen.

After I returned to Canada, I saw Sparky in Toronto on many occasions when the Detroit Tigers came to town, in the days before the present Rogers Centre was even dreamed about. His greatest delight was throwing questions at me about the game I had just watched: Why did he do that, or why didn't he throw that kind of pitch, or what do you imagine he was thinking when he did this or that? Mostly, I fear, my answers amused him rather than enlightened him. For who could possibly equal that master at his own game?

A year after he retired, I was in Los Angeles and decided to give him a call.

"When will you be through your work?" he asked.

"In about an hour," I said.

"I'll be there to pick you up. My wife and I want you to have supper with us."

That evening, which lasted till nearly 1 A.M., is still a wonderful memory. Sparky was so alive, so bubbling with enthusiasm, that I felt he would live forever. But it was not to be. How this man with such an incredible fountain of intelligence inside him and a memory for names and events that I have never seen equaled, could end his days suffering from Alzheimer's is beyond my understanding. But though he is gone, he has left behind the memory of a kind and gentle man who had the patience to talk to me about the game he so obviously loved.

Most of my friends are from the entertainment world. I thank my lucky stars that it was my good fortune, thanks to Jack Kent Cooke, to learn about baseball from the man I believe knew more about it than any other person on the face of this earth.

Thank you, Sparky Anderson, for making my life richer by giving me the opportunity to have you as my friend.

WHERE DO TODAY'S STARS
GET THEIR NAMES?

Why on earth would a talented entertainer like rapper Snoop Lion ever choose such a weird name? I realize that back in the glory days of Hollywood it was common practice to adopt names that were short enough to put on theatre marquees. It is easy to see why the great John Wayne, who was born Marion Morrison, changed his name. It took MGM studio boss Louis B. Mayer five minutes to sign a contract with Spangler Arlington Brugh as "Robert Taylor." Mayer had already changed his own name from Mayerinski to Mayer. (If you check on the Internet, you will find Louie Mayer credited with having several different birth surnames, including Meir. But to this day I am firm in my memory that he told me personally it was Mayerinski. He even spelled it out for me. So don't believe everything the Internet tells you.) Sam Goldwyn, the "G" in Metro-Goldwyn-Mayer, was once Samuel Goldfish. But Mayer's biggest success was surely renaming Greta Lovisa Gustafsson as "Greta Garbo."

I do know how one rock singer—who later changed his style and became a major star in the world of country music—got his name, because he and I chose it after a record company rejected his demo record, telling him, "The sound was good but that name will never sell anything."

When Harold Jenkins walked into my office at the CKEY radio station in Toronto in 1958, I listened to his story. Harold told me that he and his five-piece rock band had made a demo record but couldn't sell it anywhere. He and his band were playing small clubs in the Toronto area. People liked the sound, but the name Harold Jenkins somehow turned them off.

Harold Jenkins was very personable man. He had an easy style and a beautiful southern accent, and when I listened to the 45 rpm demo disc I was astonished that, regardless of the singer's name, the record was not already number one on the best-sellers charts.

As we were listening, the owner of CKEY, Jack Kent Cooke, walked into my office. He listened with us. "That's a hit," said Jack. "Is anyone using it yet, any other station?"

"No, sir," said Harold. "I can't get a record company to issue it."

"I'll fix that for you," said Jack—a major influence in the making of stars, including Paul Anka, in the early rock 'n' roll era. "I have a friend at Quality Records here in Toronto. He distributes the MGM label. It's perfect for them. I'll talk to him today and I'll drive you out to Quality tomorrow morning. If I can't get you a contract, nobody can."

He turned to me. "We've got a star here Charlie, But he'll have to change that name. "Harold Jenkins" is no good. Come up with something that nobody will ever forget. I'll need the new name when I take Mr. Jenkins to Quality tomorrow."

Jack Kent Cooke left, taking the demo record with him. Harold looked at me. "Well, what do you say we get working?" he said. "I need a new name right now."

We talked for more than an hour, throwing names back and forth, but nothing seemed remotely suitable. Harold Jenkins's vocal style sounded at times very much like Elvis Presley's, but we didn't want to try to cash in on a similar name. I ordered coffee and a couple of sandwiches at lunchtime. We agreed to have a break to refresh our thoughts. Harold opened the paperback he was reading and suggested that if he read a few pages, it might give him a new train of thought.

"What's the book?" I asked.

"It's about a spy they gave this impossible name: Edwin Twitty. Can you imagine a spy called Twitty?"

"No," I said, "but I can imagine a singer called Twitty. No one would believe it at first, but I think it would catch on."

"Twitty," said Harold. "You think? Doesn't sound too good to me, but we've gotta come up with something. 'Harold Twitty'—no, that's no good."

"Then let's cut out the "Harold'," I said. "Harold, where do you come from in the States?"

"Place you've never heard of," he said. "So small we only have one stoplight, but it doesn't work. Nearest big place is called Conway—that's in Arkansas."

And that is how Harold Jenkins became Conway Twitty.

When Conway Twitty came to the Moncton Coliseum in 1971, he made my participation in his name change official. By that time, he had become one of the world's most renowned and in-demand country singers. Loretta Lynn once said, after singing a duet with him, "There will never be another country singer like Conway. He is the supreme star." Of course, I knew he was coming to the Coliseum in Moncton, but after twelve years I wasn't even going to see him perform. People in show business are apt to forget their early days, and I feared Conway might not even remember who I was.

On the day of the concert, I was visiting a record store in Moncton when I heard my named shouted from the middle of a crowd of people. The caller was Conway Twitty, who was being mobbed by people asking for autographs.

"Get over here," he yelled. "Haven't seen you in years. Nobody knew where you had gone." He threw his arms around me. "We need to talk. Tried to find you many times," he said. "Bring your wife, we'll have dinner before the show and I'll have the best seats in the house for you."

The show was, as usual for Conway Twitty, sold out; but somehow we had the centre front-row seats. For more than a dozen years, and although he had changed from rock to country, Conway had made a point of singing the first song he ever recorded—the song he'd brought to my office—as the finale of every concert he played. That night, instead of going straight into the number to end the show, he came to the front of the stage, microphone in hand, and said these words: "Had it not been for a good friend in the audience tonight, you would have been listening not to Conway Twitty, but Harold Jenkins. He also convinced the renowned Jack Kent Cooke to get me a recording contract, and it was Mr. Cooke's station, CKEY, in Toronto, that made my first song into a hit that spread fast all over North America, Europe, and Australia—even Japan. Stand up, Charlie Foster. I owe it all to you!"

Then he sang his first big hit, "It's Only Make Believe."

After MGM signed Conway he dropped into CKEY with a new demo of the song, which he signed. I still have it to this day. It was his first autograph as Conway Twitty. After the Moncton concert, we met a few times more before he died—much too young and at the height of his career—after taking ill on his tour bus while travelling between two concerts in the southern United States.

Loretta Lynn was right. There will never be another man like Harold Jenkins—or Conway Twitty—which is a shame in today's world, where scandals, not talent, often make the headlines.

YOU MUST WORK TO MAKE CHRISTMAS MERRY

Christmas should be one of the best times of the year. But in early December of 1960, it was looking rather dismal for me. I was working in Hollywood on my first television show as a writer, when news came just three weeks before Christmas that the network was not renewing the series and no new segments would be filmed in the new year.

In 1959 I had been invited to California by actor Dennis O'Keefe to be a writer on his new half-hour television comedy, appropriately called *The Dennis O'Keefe Show*. We did our best, but everyone from Dennis down knew the format and the cast (and probably my writing) just weren't good enough to keep the show on the air.

So Christmas fifty-three years ago was looking far from happy. When the show was cancelled, so were our paychecks. Today the writers of half-hour comedies can ask for and get as much as ten thousand US dollars per segment. Then we were getting only three hundred Of course, living was much cheaper, but three hundred dollars didn't leave much for saving, and I knew I had to do something if I wanted to avoid a Christmas disaster.

I have always said I would take any job rather than be unemployed, and throughout my entire life, I have never once had to claim an unemployment cheque. But back in 1960, I hadn't worked long enough in the United States to have the right to an unemployment cheque, and it was obvious I had to find another job quickly.

Actor Richard (Dick) Gardner, who had once been the star of such major films as *The Young Lion,* had in the past two years fallen on hard times because of a few personal problems. But he was a good friend, and we saw a lot of each other in those days, when Hollywood was still a great place in which to live and work. It was Dick who suggested the solution to a bleak Christmas: a suggestion that actually led us both to success in our careers, although his was not in the entertainment industry as an actor. He proposed we hire a truck, attach it to the back of my car, and fill the truck full of Christmas trees, which we could buy very cheaply in the San Fernando Valley. If I recall correctly all these years later, we bought some very fine-looking specimens for only two dollars a tree.

We had decided on our market: where better than Beverly Hills? There should be enough money there to buy the trees. At ten dollars a tree, we would make eight dollars profit. Take out a couple dollars for the truck rental and gas, and that would leave us with three dollars each from every sale. We figured that if we could sell a couple hundred trees, the six hundred dollars each would see us through Christmas and into the new year, when writing and acting jobs might become a little easier to find.

Did we sell our two hundred trees? By working twelve hours a day I am happy to tell you that in less than ten days we actually sold seven hundred trees! We both ended our venture with over two thousand dollars in our pockets. The residents of Beverly Hills—who had no idea that we had not applied for a vendor's license and were selling the trees rather illegally—were delighted to have first-class trees brought to their doorways. I won't bore you with all the names of the rich and famous people who came to their doors in answer to our bell ringing and welcomed us with open arms. But two buyers deserve special mention—one because he helped us make a most satisfying sale to a very important person.

★

We arrived with our truckload of trees at a gorgeous home at 10957 Bellagio Drive and rang the bell. A portly gentleman answered the door. "Yes, what can I do for you good people?" he asked in the un-mistakably British voice of none other than Alfred Hitchcock.

"We would like to sell you a Christmas tree," I said.

"I don't want a Christmas tree," said Hitchcock.

Not wanting to waste time in our hectic tour of Beverly Hills and Bel Air, I began to say, "Thank you, Mr. Hitchcock, have a very merry Christmas" when he interrupted.

"Wait, my friends. I have not finished. I don't want a Christmas tree—I want three! Please, bring them in."

Dick and I carried the trees into his front hall. He told us where to put them. "I'll have them decorated today," he said. "Now, how much do I owe you?"

"Thirty dollars," said Dick.

Hitchcock pulled out his wallet and thrust a hundred-dollar bill at us. We were rather taken aback. It was early in the morning and this was only our second sale.

"Mr. Hitchcock," I said, "could we come back later for the money? Right now we don't have change for a hundred dollars.

Hitchcock looked at us and gave a snort. "Did I suggest I wanted change?" he said. "Take this and be on your way. And be sure you and your families have a very wonderful Christmas." He smiled broadly and closed the door, leaving us looking very contentedly at our hundred-dollar bill. Quite a few people gave us more than the ten dollars we asked, but Hitchcock's generosity is the memory I will never forget.

The next man I want to talk about gave me much more than dollars: he gave me a job to start on January 1, 1961.

"What are you doing selling Christmas trees?" asked the man who answered the door. He looked vaguely familiar but I didn't know why. "You are a writer. Writers should be writing, not selling Christmas trees."

I explained that the TV show I had been writing had not been renewed.

"I know that," he said. "You were working at Filmways and I saw you several times. I liked your work. Dennis O'Keefe is an old friend, but you had no hope with that cast the network gave you. My name is

Paul Henning. I own Filmways Studio. Now, what are you planning after this Christmas-tree episode ends?"

"Not sure yet," I said. "But something will come along. I don't plan to quit so soon after arriving in California. I'll find a new show."

"You just did," he said. "First let me buy a tree from you, and then let's sit down to discuss your future."

Ten minutes later I had accepted his offer to write a new show, still in early preparation, that he planned to start shooting at Filmways sometime in September 1961. It was agreed that I would be on his payroll from January 1 at $365 a week. He said he believed his new idea for a comedy would be right up my street. "But the public may not like it," he said. "We shall have to see. If it doesn't work, I have other irons in the fire. You can safely expect at least a year's work at Filmways." It turned out the public did like Paul Henning's idea for "something new," and in January I found myself working on the basic idea that became *The Beverly Hillbillies.*

My career almost came to an end when Paul asked the Screen Writers Guild to take me as a new member. They refused, saying that so many members were out of work they were not adding new members. Since the unions were very strong in Hollywood, they could dictate who worked and who didn't. It looked like my career at Filmways had ended before it began, but Paul Henning had made his decision. "You will write this show," he said. "You will be paid, and you will write, but you may not get the credit you deserve on the screen. I don't know how this will work out, but I promise it will."

And it did. I will never tell the secret of how Paul Henning beat the union, because I don't want to hurt the name of a great man who was then, and still is, revered for his generosity and his wonderful treatment of everyone who worked at his studio. But I was paid handsomely when I needed money most and that is what matters today.

When I left Filmways Paul gave me a letter listing every script I had written so I would always be able to prove I was indeed a writer on his shows. The screen credits show another name—of someone who was a union member but never wrote a single word of *The Beverly Hillbillies.*

I worked on other shows for Paul—*Mr. Ed, Green Acres* and *Petticoat Junction*—and through his contacts, got lots of extra work and extra money by supplying comedians like Bob Hope and Jack Benny with gags for their shows. Sadly, Dick didn't get any work as an actor from our Christmas venture, but because of our visit to Beverly Hills he had a very different idea that ultimately made him a very wealthy man: he noticed how many houses were up for sale in the beautiful community.

"I'm going into real estate," he said. At first he joined a major realtor, but soon after he started his own company. And even when people for whom he was selling houses offered him acting work, he only occasionally accepted; he made his satisfying life and sizeable fortune as a realtor. It was Dick who sold Lucille Ball her first home on Roxbury Drive in Beverly Hills for $160,000. (Perhaps it is just as well that he was no longer around when her daughter resold the same house for $3.5 million many years later!)

So if your Christmas isn't looking as bright as it ought to be this year, don't despair. Put on your thinking cap—as Dick Gardener did for the two of us all those years ago—be prepared to do any kind of job if it brings in a few dollars, and you may find, as we did, the end of the rainbow. It is just a matter of being, as were Dick and I, during that Christmas of 1960, in the right place at the right time. And of course, meeting a wonderful man like Paul Henning.

36

AN UNEXPECTED VISITOR
TO MY APARTMENT

I turned off the television in my Hollywood apartment in disgust on
the evening of July 12, 1960: the six o'clock news was nothing but talk
about the Democratic National Convention then taking place in Los
Angeles. I wasn't politically minded then and have never been since.
It was a very warm summer evening, and I looked out the window of
my sitting room and up at the still very blue sky tinged with red from
the setting sun in the west. Up was the only real view. My view ahead
was the unexciting wall of the apartment building next door, or along
a small passageway that ran between the two buildings.

Suddenly a window opened in the adjacent building and I was astonished to see a figure climb out into the passageway. I was just about
to call the police when the smiling young man who was now standing
close to my window, waved to me. I opened my window to hear these
words: "Would you be kind enough to help me into your apartment? I
need to get away from this place for a while."

By today's standards, my next move would be considered insane,
but the world was different then. Why I didn't ignore the plea for as-
sistance I shall never know, but I reached down, grabbed his hand,
and hauled him into my apartment. All he wore were sandals, jeans,
and a spotless Hawaiian shirt. But he had a smile that convinced me
I had nothing to fear. I wasn't acquainted with many criminals, but I
didn't imagine he looked like one.

But why was the face rather familiar? I told you politics were not my thing, and even when we shook hands and he said, "I'm Jack Kennedy," it still took me a minute to realize I was shaking hands with the man who would likely be nominated the next day as the Democratic candidate in the upcoming November federal elections.

"What on earth were you doing down there?" I asked.

"They hid me away in that apartment block hoping it would keep everyone away," he replied. "But the word spread, and the front exit of the building is totally blocked with cameras and hundreds of people. I had to get out for a while, and the window was the only exit. I didn't realize both ends of the passage are blocked with iron gates. Then I spotted you and hoped you might recognize me and give me a hand."

"I hadn't the faintest idea who you were," I said. "But you didn't look very dangerous, so I decided to listen to your explanation."

"My wife is back in Washington," said Kennedy. "She's expecting our first baby and what with being apart at such a time, plus all the ballyhoo about the election, I got desperate for a little time by myself. Do you have a car?"

"Yes, in the garage below this building. Why?"

"I want to borrow it to drive to the beach at Santa Monica, take off my shoes, and walk along the beach by myself for an hour. Will you lend it to me?"

He noticed my hesitation. "You can call my brother or my wife, if you like. They'll confirm that I won't steal the car."

I smiled. "I let you in my apartment. You tell me you are Jack Kennedy. So why should my stupidity not extend to lending you my car? Do you have a driving license?"

His jaw dropped. "Not with me, and I'm afraid I haven't got any identification," he said. "Everything is in the apartment next door and I don't want to go back there."

"OK," I said. "I think you are who you say you are, but I can't let you drive without a license. Why don't I drive you to Santa Monica? I have a Ford Galaxie convertible downstairs. You can let your hair blow in breeze. I'll drop you at the beach and park there. When you are ready to return, I'll drive you back to my apartment and you can go out the window again the way you came in."

★

Jack Kennedy left his sandals and shirt in the car and walked along the beach in solitude. He didn't ask me to accompany him and I sensed I shouldn't volunteer. Two hours later, I was asleep in the car when his voice woke me. "Sorry I was so long. It was rather like heaven walking along. Not a soul recognized me. I promise I will never forget this favour."

Back in my apartment, we talked for another hour.

"Won't they miss you next door?"

"No. I came out of my bedroom window. I told everyone that I needed sleep, was going to bed, and was not to be disturbed until I woke up."

When Barack Obama was running for the Democratic Party, he was concerned that he might not get elected because he was black. Jack Kennedy also faced the problem of trying to be a first, but in a *very* different way. "If I get the nomination tomorrow," he said, "I'll be the first Roman Catholic to try for the presidency. What do you think? Will that be against me?"

"I'm not a Catholic," I said, "but I think they'll care only about whether you will you make a good president. Do you think you can you win the nomination tomorrow?"

He told me about his opponent, Lyndon Baynes Johnson, but was convinced he could win. "If I make this hurdle and win the presidency, I want you to be the first person officially invited to my inauguration in Washington next January," he said. "Do you accept?"

"Yes, Mr. President," I said. "I'll be there!"

At this moment my doorbell rang. "Do you want to get out before I open the door?" I asked. "No," he said. "It's too peaceful here. If he's a friend of yours, he won't tell the world where I am."

But it wasn't a man at all. It was a young lady I had become very friendly with in England, when I became her publicist for a film she was making with Laurence Olivier. It was at that moment that John F. Kennedy, soon to become the thirty-fifth president of the United States, first met and talked with Marilyn Monroe.

★

It was after midnight before the party broke up. I wasn't in the conversation much after Marilyn arrived. They exchanged personal phone numbers, but Jack Kennedy did remember to ask for mine too before leaving through the window. Did I start something that had a tragic ending? I have no doubt I really do know what happened to Marilyn on that sad day she was murdered. Yes, it was unquestionably murder, but it isn't Jack Kennedy who was to blame. There have been so many stories about Marilyn's death and only one has ever come close to the truth. But I believe their meeting in my apartment triggered the murder.

The next day, John F. Kennedy was nominated as the Democratic candidate for the November election. As the world knows, he did become the first Roman Catholic president of the United States on Tuesday, November 8, 1961, when he defeated the Republican incumbent vice-president, Richard Nixon. It was the closest presidential contest of the twentieth century, but Jack Kennedy won.

I attended the inauguration, because the invitation President Kennedy had promised arrived in a registered letter together with a personal note that said simply, "Thank You. Jack." And I was close enough to the podium to hear him speak and swear his allegiance to his nation. He winked at me once as if to acknowledge our little secret, but whether that secret was his visit to my apartment or the introduction to Marilyn, we will never now know. We spoke on the phone a few times after that. I found that giving my name to the White House switchboard, as he suggested, got me right through to him. He certainly hadn't forgotten me.

Despite his personal failings, John F. Kennedy was, in my opinion, a good man, and probably one of the greatest presidents the United States has ever known. But I recall him simply as Jack Kennedy, the man who, at a special moment in his life, desperately needed time to himself. I feel content today that I was able to give him that time.

WHY ON EARTH ARE YOU
LIVING IN NEW BRUNSWICK?

That is a question I have been asked many times. After the glamour of London and Hollywood, why did I choose New Brunswick as my final destination to live and work?

When the drug dealers began to arrive on the Hollywood scene in the late 1950s, I saw many of my friends destroy their lives. I wanted none of this, and when an offer came to write a Canadian comedy series I jumped at the chance to move to Toronto. Though the series collapsed when the creators found they could not get backers, I decided to stay in the city.

I became features editor of the *Brampton Daily Times* and since it was owned by the *Toronto Telegram*, I wrote many stories in the 1960s for that paper too. A move to be editor of *Stage Door*—a weekly entertainment magazine devised by James Colistro, a choreographer who had worked for many stars, including Anne Murray—should have been a great thing, but Jimmy ran out of money and the magazine shut its doors.

In 1970, Bill Doole—a friend of mine and former publisher of the *Brampton Daily Times*—knowing I was at loose ends, said he had heard that the editor of a weekly paper in New Brunswick, the *Moncton Free Press*, had died suddenly, and that the owners, Vaughan Harvey and Cy Spear, were in need of help.

"Have you ever heard of Moncton?" asked Bill.

"Heard of it?" I said. "I love the city. I had the good fortune to be there during the Second World War when I was in the RAF."

"Then there is a job waiting for you there," he said.

And that is how I returned to Moncton in 1970. The job was to be for six weeks. But I am still here.

★

The paper had little hope of surviving. It was created as an attack on the mayor of the city, Leonard C. Jones, by two of his former council members. Since everyone but Cy Spear and Vaughan Harvey liked Jones, despite his controversial nature, it was tough for them to get advertisers and after six months they closed their doors. Within days of arriving I, too, decided I liked what Len Jones was doing for the city, so wasn't unhappy about the closure.

My wife and I decided to stay. We bought the house that we still live in today, and I started my own monthly entertainment newspaper, *Entertainment Atlantic*, which I ran successfully for two years before I got an offer I couldn't refuse. The federal government offered me a job writing feature articles for magazines and speeches for members of the federal cabinet. In ten years, I wrote for three prime ministers and hundreds of members of the cabinet. Since I had, from the start, refused to write political rubbish—only simply speeches that told the facts—I survived three successive governments.

Then I was given the chance to write my first book. Keith Lyne—head of communications in the Halifax office of the federal Department of Regional Industrial Expansion—asked me if I thought I could put in book form the history of Nova Scotia's forestry industry. The result was *The Trees Around Us*, which now has a place of pride in my library, and actually became a very successful book in Atlantic Canada.

Two years before I retired at sixty-five, I won a government award as the best speechwriter in Canada; to this day, the certificate hangs on the wall of my home.

One of my favourite moments working for the federal government came following a speech I wrote for Prime Minister Pierre Trudeau. Mr. Trudeau had decided to bring his entire cabinet to Nova Scotia for an official meeting, and he wanted a speech for the public occasion that was to open that session. To my delight, I was invited to Ottawa to discuss the situation with the prime minister. The two of us had a thirty-minute session that was much more humorous and friendly than I had expected. The rules were very simple: he wanted a speech that would let people know he appreciated the assets of Atlantic Canada and that its people were always on his mind. There were a few other rules that seemed a little stringent, but this was my first prime ministerial speech, so I didn't argue. His office had to have a phone number at which I could be reached twenty-four hours a day. Remember, this was before cellphones. If I went to the theatre, or even out for supper, I had to call an Ottawa number and leave them contact information.

I must report that not once was I called at any of my locations, and apparently when I sent along my draft speech it was approved. I didn't hear a word from the prime minister, and when he and the cabinet arrived in Nova Scotia I was still in my office in Moncton and not even invited to the sessions.

The night of the meeting I heard nothing. I was fast asleep in bed at 2 A.M. when my bedside phone rang.

"Charles?" said a voice.

"Yes," I said. "Who on earth is calling at this time of night?"

"It's Pierre," said the voice.

"Pierre? Pierre who?" I asked, still not quite awake.

"Pierre Elliot Trudeau, your prime minister," said the voice.

"Oops," I said. "Sorry sir. Didn't expect you to call!"

"Sorry I'm so late," said Mr. Trudeau. "Just got back to my room in the hotel after one of the most enjoyable evenings of my life. I want you to know that the speech you wrote was excellent. In fact, I want to put it quite clearly: it is probably one of the best of my entire career. You did me a lot of good tonight and I shall not forget that. Even though it is so late, I want to officially invite you to join my staff in Ottawa as a speechwriter. What do you say?"

"Sir," I said, "I'd need to think about it. I love my home in New Brunswick. I enjoy what I am doing here. No—I won't even think about it. Much as I am delighted with your comments and your invitation, I must reject the offer. I am going to stay here in New Brunswick for the rest of my life."

"You don't want to think about my offer?" was the reply.

"No, sir! I am wide awake now and know what I am saying."

"Then good night and thank you for making my visit so successful." The prime minister hung up the phone. I did receive a letter from him repeating his offer a week later but I did not change my decision. Sadly, I never did get another request to write for Mr. Trudeau. I still have letters from two other prime ministers, more than thirty cabinet members, and other lowly politicians, thanking me for the speeches I wrote for them.

After retirement I wrote for the *County Chronicle*, a weekly newspaper based in my hometown, Riverview, New Brunswick, and sold hundreds of stories to magazines around the world. I wrote three books, two of which—*Stardust and Shadows* and *Once Upon A Time In Paradise*—were bestsellers. The third, *Donald Brian, King of Broadway*, was a regional publication in the Newfoundland market that was successfully adapted into a musical production in St. John's. The Moncton *Times and Transcript* asked me to write a twenty-part history of the newly reopened Capitol Theatre in Moncton, and later I became the writer of a seniors' paper, *Young At Heart*, which ran successfully in the *Times and Transcript* for several months. For the past nine years, I have contributed my memories to the *Seniors Advocate* in Nova Scotia, and each month I receive hundreds of emails from readers who seem to enjoy the stories.

So I learned all over again to love New Brunswick and Atlantic Canada, and knew I had made the best decision of my life by moving back here in 1970. But what happened back during the Second World War that made me think this was the greatest city in Canada? I must tell you that story before I end this book.

TⱯE ᴚAF LET ME DISCOVER
A WⱯOLE NEW WORLD

In 1943, after an uneventful trip across the Atlantic from England in
the Cunard liner *Queen Elizabeth*, several hundred hopeful pilots and
I arrived in Moncton by a train that took us right into the grounds
of what we soon discovered was No. 31 Personnel Dispatch Centre
(31PDC) . At first we were told we would be in Moncton for about two
weeks but that estimate was extended due to a measles epidemic that
swept through the base. We were there for almost five weeks. There
were many things to do in the city, and residents were generous in asking us to visit their homes, but we were getting very bored. Everyone
of us wanted to get on with our flying training.

There were a few unhappy incidents, and Group Captain Carleton,
our base commanding officer (CO), decided to step in and help reduce
the tension. He asked if anyone on the base had any involvement in
the theatre prior to enlisting, so I volunteered, without any idea what
he was planning. Having been a band booker and a stagehand at the
Theatre Royal in Stockport, I ambitiously decided that my experience
classified me as a near professional. I remember also telling the CO
how when I was only ten, I had written a play for the BBC *Children's
Hour* in England.

With co-operation from Radio CKCW in Moncton, the decision
was made to broadcast a thirty-minute radio show directly from the
camp theatre. They really didn't expect anything of great quality,
but hoped it would give those involved something to do. Obviously

nobody cared if we spread our measles to the employees of the radio station who had come to the camp, but happily that did not happen. Our show was to be called *Thirty Minutes At Thirty One*.

For some reason I can't explain to this day, I was chosen to produce the show. I can only presume that my meagre experience was in excess of that of other volunteers. My contact at CKCW was Bert Hebert, a sound engineer who went out of his way to make sure we had everything we wanted. I mention this great gentleman because, many years later, I had the pleasure to meet him again when I was talking to George Hebert, the fabulous guitarist who became famous for his contribution to Anne Murray's rise to international success. George was Bert Hebert's son.

I was approached by Pilot Officer James "Jimmy" Keith O'Neill Edwards, a recent pilot graduate waiting to be sent home to England. He wanted to be part of the show. "I don't know what I can do," said Jimmy, "but I think I can be a comedian." Given his round, happy face and huge handlebar moustache, I agreed. I discovered that he planned to be a teacher after the war. So somehow I wrote a comedy sketch using Jimmy in his chosen profession as a rather unusual teacher, and remarkably, it turned out to be a huge hit. It was such a hit for Jimmy that five years after the war, he was still using it in the British music halls.

We broadcast many acceptable singers and one a former opera tenor, and added a couple of local ladies who worked at the base to take part in sketches. I wrote other skits, and even used some tap dancers from a local dancing school. But, reluctantly, we had to turn down our one real music hall professional—a juggler who had worked in the best theatres in England and Europe—because we couldn't figure out how a juggler could be successful on radio.

But *Thirty Minutes At Thirty One* was more than just a half-hour wonder. Moncton Mayor Frank Storey heard the show and asked Group Captain Carleton if he would permit the performers to stage a full two-hour version of it at Moncton's Capitol Theatre. He suggested the show could run for three nights, with all the money raised going to a wartime charity.

The CO asked me, and Jimmy, who had been such a hit on the radio, if we thought such a live show was possible. We agreed to do it if we were allowed to enlist the aid of ten local musicians to form a pit orchestra to accompany the singers and dancers. I was officially made producer, writer, and general slave for the two weeks we were given to prepare everything. It was night-and-day work. Everyone involved on the base was released from other duties to help. This included cleaning the Capitol stage, which hadn't been used for live shows in years.

Under the stage, we found trunks and scenery left behind by vaudeville shows that apparently had gone bankrupt. In the trunks were costumes, which a local dressmaker worked on for hours so we could use them. Volunteers from the city came in to help clean the dilapidated scenery we'd discovered. An electrician in town set up superb lighting for us, and soon the movie theatre was ready for its first live show in a decade.

A thirty-year-old American film actor, Phillips Holmes—who had made more than twenty films before volunteering for the RAF—was stationed at the nearby Scoudouc flying school where he had been Jimmy Edwards's flying instructor. Jimmy asked Holmes if he would help, and Holmes's knowledge about staging a production went a long way toward making the show the success it eventually turned out to be.

The Capitol Theatre's owner, Fred Winter, gave us total co-operation, and on opening night the show received eight curtain calls. Little did they know, it had almost had a disastrous ending.

★

Just three minutes before the scheduled finale, Herbert Brownbill—our tenor who had sung with the Sadler's Wells Opera Company in London—whispered to me that he had developed laryngitis and there was no way he could possibly sing *There'll Always Be An England* in the closing scene. We had other singers in the show, but nobody with the voice of Herbert Brownbill. I was considering what to do when I felt a tap on my shoulder. A young aircrew trainee—who had been playing parts in skits because he had a remarkably resonant voice that had attracted our attention—said, "I can tackle the song. I know I'm not as good as Bert, but I can do it."

There was no other option. I told Dick Jenkins to get ready to go onstage.

"Don't worry," he said. "I really have quite a good singing voice and I know the words and the song well. I won't let you down. I was just starting my career as an actor when I joined the RAF, so I have a bit of stage training."

Dick Jenkins certainly didn't let us down. He raised his rich baritone voice in the finale with such astonishing success that he had the audience on its feet, cheering and applauding, before he had finished the first chorus. Twice the audience demanded he repeat the song, and I saw tears streaming down his face as he came offstage after the final curtain.

It was then that Mayor Frank Storey stepped onstage. "This has been an unforgettable night in my life," he said. "Moncton welcomes members of the RAF to our city and I want you to know that all 1,400 seats at each of the next two shows are already sold. This is my official request to Group Captain Carleton that two more shows be added."

Our commanding officer joined the mayor onstage. "Mr. Mayor, if the theatre is available, my men are ready. And I hope the young ladies from the city who have joined them onstage will also be ready, in which case we are willing to extend the show to five nights." Fred Winter, the Capitol's owner, then walked onstage. "I will cancel two films," he said. "The theatre is yours."

We made a lot of money for the charity, and on the final night the mayor came back onstage, carrying an engraved plaque to commemorate the occasion. He handed it to the CO, who had attended every performance. The plaque was placed on the wall of the base theatre at No. 31 and everyone stationed at the base looked at it with pride. Then one day, it suddenly disappeared. There was a huge outcry and the military police combed the base looking for it. But it never turned up.

Our finale singer, Dick Jenkins, became the toast of the town. When we took over a complete floor of the Brunswick Hotel a week later for a party to celebrate the success, Dick had so many girls lining up to kiss him that the rest of us were more than a little jealous. Little did these girls know that they were kissing a major star of the future. After the war Dick Jenkins changed his name legally and became none other than superstar Richard Burton.

Some years after the war, I visited Dick in his London home. He was very proud of his recreation room and its full-sized billiard room. But I was more intrigued with what I saw hanging on the wall behind the table. It was the plaque Mayor Frank Storey had presented to us on the final night of our successful stage show in Moncton. I pointed to it in astonishment. "Yes," said Dick, "I stole it. I thought I had earned it that night and might never again achieve success like that."

"Where on earth did you hide it?" I asked. "Security searched every inch of the base."

"I shall never tell," said Dick. "It was in one of the most visible places at No. 31, but because it was so obvious, nobody spotted it."

To this day, I have no idea where it was hidden at No. 31. And while I do know where it is today, I'm not going to tell that secret.

EPILOGUE

If you think I have forgotten to keep a promise I made in the prologue, you are wrong.

I am finally going to tell you why the distinguished Canadian millionaire Lord Beaverbrook, who spent most of his early life in New Brunswick and Nova Scotia, came to be sitting next to me on a small, rocky ferry taking us from England to France way back in 1936.

I had rather unexpectedly won a scholarship to Buxton College in Derbyshire, England, when I was only eleven and by 1936, at thirteen, had achieved success as an athlete without hurting my scholastic work. Despite this success, only a few months later, when the Fossett's Circus and Billy Smart's lions came to town, I left with them.

As a boarding student in Burlington House at Buxton College, I was already on the college soccer and cricket teams playing with boys eighteen and nineteen years old. I was house champion at singles tennis and at boxing, I had won the approval of everyone when I knocked out the school bully in the third round of a bout nobody expected me to win. But it was my success as a runner that brought me attention from outside the confines of the college. Don McLaren, our athletic director, watched me win both the one hundred- and two hundred-yard sprints at the college's annual sports day and entered me in the provincial college championships.

When I astonished everyone by winning those too, Mr. McLaren got permission from my parents to enter me in the county championships at nearby Chesterfield. There, I was to compete against the top amateurs of all ages. I can see to this day the look of amazement on the face of the man handing out the medals in Chesterfield when they gave me the gold in both the one hundred- and two hundred-yard sprints. Even though they were standing on lower levels, the second- and third-place winners towered over my head.

So with my race figures looking very good, I caught the eye of whoever Lord Beaverbrook had hired to choose the thirty young British athletes who were to travel with him, at his expense, to see the 1936 Olympic Games in Berlin, Germany. All those chosen to go to Berlin were considered prospects for the 1940 Olympics in Tokyo, Japan.

Lord Beaverbrook himself had called my parents to get their approval for the trip after discovering how young I was in contrast to the other twenty-nine men and women selected. They had approved, once he promised to personally look after me during the two-week visit to Berlin. Lord Beaverbrook kept his promise. Throughout the entire journey by train and boat, he had me sit beside him so he could be certain no harm came to me. My conversations with him were many and fascinating.

Of course a little war intervened and there were no 1940 Olympics. There were none in 1944 either, and when they did resume in 1948 I was certainly no candidate. I hadn't run in years—although I must put on record that during my RAF pilot training in 1943 in Medicine Hat, I did win the one hundred yards (or was it metres then?) at 34 Service Flying Training School.

But the 1936 games cannot be ignored. They were the games at which the incredible Jesse Owens showed the world that black athletes are second to none. Even though Hitler, who was present, managed to be absent at all his medal presentations, Jesse Owens went down in the world's sporting records in a way no other man has since equalled. It was my good luck to receive a handshake from Owens as he jogged past the luxury stand on which the thirty future athletes from England sat. And I still recall being introduced to a German athlete, Lutz Long, who fell out of favour with Hitler because he actually embraced the victorious Jesse Owens.

We were all horrified by Hitler's treatment of Owens, but I must put on record something I learned from Owens himself many years later, when it was my privilege to be his publicity representative on a visit he made to England with the Harlem Globetrotters. He told me that he was quite used to being ignored. "In the United States, back in 1936, there was still considerable discrimination against black people," he said. "I didn't find that in Berlin. There, for the first time in my life, I was welcomed into the best restaurants, and thousands of friendly Germans patted me on the back and crowded round for autographs. People didn't shake hands with blacks in America then, no matter what they achieved."

Jesse Owens won four gold medals in the sprint and long-jump categories. It was in the long jump that he competed against Lutz Long. At our meeting years later, Owens told me he won that event because Long, who spoke good English, actually told him what he was doing wrong and how he could correct his run before making the jump. "It was Lutz who let me take away the gold medal—he took silver in that event," Owens said.

I never did meet Lord Beaverbrook again after that wonderful visit to Berlin, but to this day I am delighted to say that it was his proud comments about Canada—Atlantic Canada in particular—that helped make me a permanent resident and citizen of this great country.

I turned ninety in January of 2013, and hope to still be around when the queen sends me the official letter that all centenarians receive on reaching one hundred. Who knows—by then the queen may well be the granddaughter of the wonderful flying instructor I was privileged to know back in 1943 in Calgary. For I will always believe it was Peter Middleton who made my entire happy life possible.

Now, wouldn't that make a wonderful finale?